CAN I BE ME?

LIVING

AUTHENTICALLY

IN PURPOSE

ON PURPOSE

CHERYL LACEY DONOVAN

To
My Daughter Brandy

Love You To Life

Always Be You.

Duchess

Can I Be Me?

ISBN-13: 978-1719422055   ISBN-10: 1719422052

Peace in the Storm Publishing, LLC

Visit our Website at: www.peaceinthestormpublishing.com

Disclaimer: This publication is for informational purposes only and is not intended as medical advice. Medical advice should always be obtained from a qualified medical professional for any health conditions or symptoms associated with them. Every possible effort has been made in preparing and researching this material. We make no warranties with respect to the accuracy, applicability of its contents or any omissions.

Acknowledgments

God is just so amazing! He loves us in spite of us. He gives us the time we need to truly become who He has called us to be. Finding identity and purpose in Him is the ultimate outcome of living authentically in purpose and on purpose.

Elissa Gabrielle is more than a publisher. She is a friend, a confidant, a sister. Her leadership at Peace in the Storm Publishing has been phenomenal. I am grateful to have her in my life.

To my family, I love you and thank you for being on this journey with me.

Contents

Limited Special Offer:

Can I Be Me? Living Authentically in Purpose on Purpose Course

Cheryl Lacey Donovan

INTRODUCTION

Are you tired of living behind a mask? Tired of living up to everyone else's expectations but your own? Are you ready to live authentically in purpose on purpose?

When you become a woman of a certain age there comes a time when after being all things to all people, you stop to wonder, "Can I finally just be me?"

Working a regular 9 to 5 job and spending time climbing your way up the career ladder can be satisfying, but the process can become tiresome and tedious. You find yourself wondering if you've lost sight of the important things in life.

AUTHENTIC MOMENT: Has it all been worth it, has anyone even cared or noticed the effort I've been making? People noticing, is that even a rational reason to put forth the effort in the first place? Is life only about living up to the expectations of others?

Does any of this sound familiar?

I've spent a lifetime concerned about everyone else's expectations and now I'm empty. A life altering epiphany for sure, but now, I need to listen to my own heart and take better care of myself. It's now or never. I must speak my own truth, listen to my own voice, or I can just continue to fit into a prefabricated existence designed by architects who have no insight into the master's plan.

Ready to embrace a life that's reflective of my own dreams and desires, I remember thinking, "I'm tired of responding to everyone else's needs and neglecting my own."

Even my husband reminded me of how I never take the time to buy anything new for myself. I quipped, "I must be the only woman in the world whose husband is mad that she doesn't spend enough money on herself."

Like everyone, I've been blessed with great talents and inspirations capable of driving me forward in life, but I have never really taken all the necessary steps to fully realize my longings and ideas so, it's no wonder that my passion for life declined. I had become accustomed to ignoring my own hopes in lieu of fulfilling the hopes others had for me. It can be defeating to spend your life working toward essentially nothing, destined to repeat the same monotonous routines while the things you really want to do with your life is stuck on the back burner.

That's no way to live, but many of us are stuck and confined as we wonder about the things that might have been, were we offered better opportunities, or had we found more time to work on the things most important to us. Unfortunately, the answer to living authentically may escape us for a lifetime if we never choose to stop and ask ourselves who we are and what story we want our lives to tell.

I am a Wife, a Mother, a Daughter, a Friend, a Minister, Mentor, etc. etc. etc. Not too bad in and of themselves. But I was me before I was a mother, I was me before I was a wife, and I was me before I was a friend. Who am I really without all the titles? Who, am I at my core?

Other people's expectations can override your understanding of God's expectations as well as your own. The result, an inauthentic lifestyle of someone else's making. When your truth is altered, you look like someone you don't even recognize. You walk through life a watered-down version of yourself that everyone else feels comfortable with except you. "What if," you ask yourself. I know I'm not the only woman who has the desire to find purpose beyond the roles that I play. So, with this book as a guide, I hope to help us all realize there is no reason to wonder "what if?" any more. I want us to take this journey together as we learn how to uncover the selves we have hidden behind a mask for so long. I want to share my story and hopefully hear your story as we reconnect with ourselves and learn that it is not only possible, but essential, that we live our lives authentically. Stagnant marriages, demanding children, empty nests, bad bosses, lackluster careers, it doesn't matter, God created every one of us with a special life assignment and a singular life that belongs to us and us alone. Each of us has a duty to honor the life assignment we were meant to complete openly, honestly, and without shame. It is up to us to create the changes that need to be made to make living authentically a reality.

Single mothers, married women, divorced women, widowed women, young mothers, daughters, sisters, aunts, grandmothers, and friends, if you're desperate and courageous enough, we can walk together and do the work to live a life of authenticity. I will provide a basic structure and guidance to help you learn to be in the present, deviate from the beaten path, learn to care for yourself, and not be a fraud in your own life. Accomplishing this may seem obscure and idealistic at first, but I encourage you not to spend one more day being a stranger to yourself. Find out what it means to live authentically, learn to accept yourself and love yourself as you are, develop the courage to be yourself around others, understand your value and what you have to offer, discover your passions and how to enjoy them daily, and embrace your individuality.

By beginning the journey of authentic living, I have been able to experience major accomplishment sin my life. From becoming a best –selling award winning author, to running building and running a media company, to accessing some of gospel music's biggest celebrities on the red carpet as a media personality, none of this would have been possible without accessing who I am. It has not been easy, and I am still on my journey but if your desire is to live in your truth, refresh your spirit, resurrect those parts of yourself that have been buried for years, or to simply breathe again, then now is the time and this is the book. But, let me warn you, you must do the work. It will take discipline, determination, and time but by following the simple suggestions in this book, before you know it you will be well on your way to living authentically in purpose on purpose!

Don't put off for tomorrow what you can do today. Do it now before it is too late. Be the person who is motivated to act without hesitation.

Your time under God is now, so, let's get started.

Cheryl Lacey Donovan

NOTES

IDENTITY THEFT

I am chosen and appointed by God to bear his fruit. John 15:16

Identity theft is the deliberate use of someone else's identity, usually as a method to gain a financial advantage or obtain credit and other benefits in the other person's name, and perhaps to the other person's disadvantage or loss.

It's crazy to think but how, many of us have lived identities for the monetary gain, creditability and/or benefit of someone else only to learn we're frauds in our own lives. We've allowed others to make withdrawals from our identity by allowing them to tell us what we couldn't do or by listening when they dictated what we needed to do even when it didn't align with our inner truth. Translation our identities were stolen, and our accounts are bankrupt. Self-awareness is the most important aspect of authentic living because everything else in our lives, our ability to stay the course or course correct to achieve our goals is determined by what we know about who we are. As you peel away the layers of your soul, you'll discover some wonderful things about yourself. You'll also discover some not so wonderful things. Continuing the journey of self-awareness will require courage and perseverance because it may get ugly sometimes. Our good qualities are easy to deal with. It's the bad ones for which justification of our negative thoughts and behaviors but one way to cultivate awareness of them we must look deep into ourselves. Truthfully and openly writing down the good and the bad leads us to a place where we can deal with the negative and accentuate the positive

AUTHENTIC MOMENT: Who knew I was self-conscious and insecure. I sure didn't. And yes, I said it here; self-conscious and insecure. There have been many times when I have walked into a room and the only thing on my mind was the perception other people would have of me. Even in ministry I often wondered if the people would respond to what I had to say. My identity in Christ has been a key component in moving forward in my journey to authentic living. After much reflection and thought I recognized I didn't need a good self-image. What I needed was the right self-image - one that came from God's Word.

How God sees us shapes our personality, our attitude, and our relationships. It's seldom that you run into anyone who was consistently taught that God sees us as His child... daughters and sons chosen by God to be included in His family. We didn't just "happen," we were intentionally adopted by God.

Everything in a Christian woman's life is built on the foundation of her identity. When the foundation is cracked everything else is on shaky ground.

I struggled with who I was and so often compared myself with other women. It was uncommon for me to come up short with who I thought I needed to be because in my mind my worth depended on what I did, what I looked like, or what others said about me instead of what God said about me.

Even though I was a PK (Preacher's Kid) I didn't know where I stood with God. I knew I was "saved", but that's about it. But as I got grounded in who God says I am, I began to experience the authentic abundant life that Jesus came to give me. Not just the monetary abundance most people think of but, abundant peace, abundant joy, abundant health and so much more.

Oh, what joy that flooded my soul when I finally got it! God sees me as His daughter. Once adopted, I can't be "un-adopted." What an exciting truth, that once fully understood has set me free to be all God created me to be!

AUTHENTIC MOMENT: I hate confrontation. Therefore, I tend to keep my thoughts to myself rather than risk hurting someone else's feelings or getting into an argument. Why is this not good? Because in the process I have often lost a piece of who I am. I lost my ability to have thoughts, opinions, and ideas that while they may be different from others, they are still mine. Because of my reluctance to assert myself I had difficulty making decisions. Blow ups weren't uncommon either because I bottled up how I felt and after a while it just became more than I could handle.

When you are self- aware, you can change deeply held beliefs when they don't serve you well. Your inner landscape is full of surprises that you can cultivate and grow what you know more about yourself.

When you become self-aware, you know your strengths, your weaknesses, and your personality type. But it's more than this. Understanding "you" requires the ability to objectively observe your thoughts without emotional attachment.

For example, you might tell yourself, "Now I'm experiencing anger." You can then go on to ask yourself why you're getting angry and where that anger is coming from. Certainly, your soul within you is not angry. So, who is?

Our inner dialogue of learning who we are requires us to take into consideration that there are many different types of people in the world with many different internal and external stimuli. One person's outlook on life may be totally different from the others even if they grow up in the same household.

…There are people who live in poverty but are internally happy and content.

…There are people who live with excessive material possessions but are completely miserable on the inside.

…There are people who desperately seek to improve everything about their lives.

…There are people who only want to change one or two things about their lives.

…There are people who feel trapped by other people's expectations and there are those trapped by *their own* expectations.

...There are even people who have absolutely no idea what they want and have completely given up hope because they have tried and tried and yet, no matter how hard they have tried they still fail.

So, as we take this journey together, I don't mind telling you a person who doesn't know themselves, inside and out, cannot grow and change in ways that will help them to evolve as a person, because that person will likely be a slave to their vices without even knowing it!

Furthermore, most of us have a hard time admitting our flaws and faults, even to ourselves. Not admitting them gives them free reign over our lives, as well as the ability to sabotage everything we do. It is a sneaky way for us to get in our own ways without really being able to see the problem for what it is; an act of self-sabotage!

Introspection is the most effective strategy I know for combating self-sabotage. This may seem simple, but I can tell you from experience it is a difficult ride. It's more than just sitting down and listing the things you think you know about yourself. Introspection is a time-intensive process that you will need to do with the help of friends and family whom you can trust to tell you the truth even if it hurts your feelings. However, the effectiveness of the process rests on your ability to understand that the only person you can change is yourself. When you choose to transform yourself, you'll notice changes in your environment, including the people who surround you. The world is your mirror and both the negative and the positive situations you encounter are created by you.

Go deeper into yourself and peel away the layers until you can see who you truly are. This is the sort of analysis and probing that will help you answer the question that great minds have asked across the centuries: "Who am I?"

AUTHENTIC MOMENT: One thing that may really help you is to take a personality test. Once you take a test, you will usually be placed in one category or another based on your answers. These categories each have a detailed profile that can help you understand more about yourself and the way you respond to certain situations and stimuli. This can also be useful in learning more about how you conduct yourself in relationships and as a part of a peer group, without having to rely on the feedback of your trusted friends and family.

Personality tests are very insightful when it comes to the way one approaches their goals and whether they are realistic in the way they attempt to achieve their dreams. Knowing your personality type may provide you with what you have been waiting for when it comes to which approach might work best for you in furthering your career or tackling the to-do list that has been put on the back burner for far too long.

Here's what one test said about me.

You tend to be very focused. You value harmony, compassion, and helping other people. You are skilled at offering sincere encouragement and support. You are uncomfortable with conflict and will work hard to prevent and/or avoid confrontations. You like to be appreciated for the warm human being you are! If you're given a job, you can be counted on to do it, to do it right, and to get it done on time. You value fairness and consistency and like clear guidelines to follow.

You need clear rules and boundaries, structure, stability, an organized environment and schedule, consistency, opportunities to show your responsibility and reliability, and time to complete a project well. You need understanding, harmony, love, acceptance, honesty, inspiration, and empathy.

You're frustrated by broken promises, negative criticism, people talking about you behind your back, conflict and confrontation, lying and rejection, lack of social opportunities, a focus on systems rather than on people, conformity that doesn't allow for individuality, lack of opportunities to talk over what's happening, and insincerity. You're frustrated by tasks left unfinished, ambiguity, chaos and disorganization, too many things going on at the same time, people who don't follow through, irresponsibility and waste, nonconformity, changing rules, the phrase "it depends", and a haphazard attitude.

With friends you really care about what happens to those who are close to you. You listen and are honest and genuine. You're dependable. You like your friends to be honest, especially about money and making plans to do things.

At home you try to keep everything in harmony. You are sensitive and like warm feelings and quiet talks. You love responsibilities and working hard. You also like a secure family life and enjoy holidays and celebrations.

Yep, that's me!

Having more clarity about my personality allowed me to narrow my attention and consider what I believe in. Knowing your values results in clarity and focus. Your values can be used to define your priorities. These priorities can determine how to best spend your time and energy. Knowing your values can greatly streamline your life and your efforts. Decisions become easier to make.

To begin to consider our lives properly, without self-delusion, without ignoring any part of our being and without neglecting any part of ourselves, we absolutely must start with open and sincere honesty.

If we are not honest with ourselves about the things we don't like, or don't want in our lives, if we are not honest about the things we want to change, then there is no way that we can ever hope to achieve true fulfilment. Why is this so? It's simple, everyone must decide what it means to live authentically for themselves. It's a personal decision.

Sure, you can seek guidance in general terms, but ultimately, it is you who must decide what works for you otherwise, how can we ever hope to make the changes necessary to live life to the fullest, instead of just accepting the status quo?

Each of us have core values that provide us with the drive that pushes us forward. If we don't know what we believe in, then it can be hard for us to feel fulfilled and our lives will lack passion and motivation. How does the saying go, "If we don't stand for something, we will fall for anything?" But once we latch onto a core value that we truly feel passionate about, everything begins to change. We can begin building a foundation for our lives and experiences based on these values; in a way that makes even the most mundane task begin to feel rewarding.

How might that be? Because when you are living a life that is true to your core values and beliefs, you begin to accomplish things that serve your life's assignment.

How can you live according to your values?

1.   Make a list of your values. write them down. It's that simple. It doesn't matter how big or how small. If, it matters to you write it down.

•   Prioritize your list. Put them in order Just from most important to least.

• Reexamine your list. Now that you have a prioritized list, decide if you're happy with it. Consider the life you'd like to live. Will your list of values get you there? Reorder your list as appropriate.

2. Use your values to choose a career or hobby.

• Does your current career line up with your values? If not, can you change careers? If you can't change careers at this point in your life, can you do something on the side that will allow you to live your values?

3. Create habits in alignment with your values.

• List any habits that are counter to your values, too.

4. Choose the people in your life. No matter how independent you might be, the people in your life influence your thoughts, decisions, and behavior.

Consider how you think and act around each of the people in your life. Consider spending less time with the people that pull you away from your values and more time with the people that push you toward your values.

- Be strong. Some of your longtime friends might be having a negative effect on your ability to be true to yourself.

5. Make decisions with your values in mind. Knowing and living your values can make your decisions much easier.

- Use your values when making decisions.

Learn and live your values. You'll be able to make decisions easier and more quickly. Life has fewer options when you're familiar with your values, and the best option will become more obvious.

AUTHENTIC MOMENT: Here are a few of the things I value. Feel free to go online and pull up a values list to assist you in identifying what is most important to you.

- Faith
- Compassion
- Fairness
- Love
- Kindness
- Meaningful work
- Peace
- Service
- Wisdom
- Stability

After reading this chapter it should be clear that, many people simply don't know themselves well enough to live an authentic life. Whether it is a traumatic past that keeps you stuck, or it is simply a lack of self-knowledge or discipline, we all must know who we are at the most fundamental level. Many people are so disconnected from themselves that they don't even know what it is they like or dislike. So, take a moment to introduce yourself to you.

If you have a hard time with this, now is the time to trust your friends and family to help you see yourself objectively. Consider their opinions on the flaws, weaknesses, and vices that you might need to address. Honesty about these weaknesses helps you to deal with them so that they are no longer holding you back. Be creative and find ways to build them into strengths!

Goal: *Start a journal. In this journal, outline the things that make you who you are. Write down your self-perception in as much detail as possible. Take a test online to find out your Personality type, and journal about any insights you might have learned from taking this test.*

Every day, write about a strength in yourself you have used recently and how it is positively impacting your life. Also, write about a weakness in yourself that you have pinpointed, and what you are doing to address it and balance it out so that you are taking control over your vices and turning them into strengths! A person with power over their own faults is a person living authentically.

Cheryl Lacey Donovan

NOTES

Why You Should Find Your Passion and Follow It

How does your life make you feel? Do you wake each morning looking forward to the day ahead or do you wish you could bury your head under the covers and stay there? Your answer to this question will depend on whether there is something in your life for which you have a passion.

What is Passion?

Passion is a strong and compelling desire for someone or something that inspires you and ultimately creates happiness.

Why Do You Need Passion?

Without passion in your life you will probably find that your days often feel dull and boring. There may be a sense of something missing or lacking. You might also feel tired and depressed. Passion for life can create enormous change. Finding it makes you look forward to the day ahead. You'll want to get out of bed in the morning and you'll have more energy, focus, and creativity that will inspire to follow your dreams and create goals.

A passion for life will also help you create better relationships with family, friends and colleagues because they will respond to your positive energy and enthusiasm.

Passion in life can also create passion in work. When this happens, a huge shift can take place because now rather than simply existing in your work you are now undertaking work that you love as well. Wouldn't it feel amazing to earn an income from doing something that inspires you and brings you joy?

Finding passion for something can create an enormous transition in your life and emotions. It can help you live a fulfilling life where every day brings purpose, energy, commitment and achievement. If life feels dull, uninspiring and leaves you with little energy and focus then why not look for that something, a cause, hobby or career, that feels right and sparks joy within you? You'll be amazed at the difference it makes to you, your relationships and possibly, your finances.

AUTHENTIC MOMENT: Healthcare is an industry that will always be around. If there are people, there will be a need for doctors, nurses, allied health care professionals, etc. This is one of the reasons I was guided to the profession. That and the death of a cousin from breast cancer when I was younger.

However, years later after being wrongfully released from a position I had maintained for five years (read one of my other books to find out why) I stumbled upon something I truly loved; teaching. Who knew? Well, apparently many of the people I grew up with because several of them have told me about how I use to line them up to play school. Go figure.

My gift for teaching has spawned into areas I had no idea I would ever experience: writing, speaking, creating personal development courses, and preaching to name a few.

This is what gives me joy. Creating and re-creating in this area is what brings my soul joy! It's my passion and I am grateful to have identified it.

Can I Be Me?

NOTES

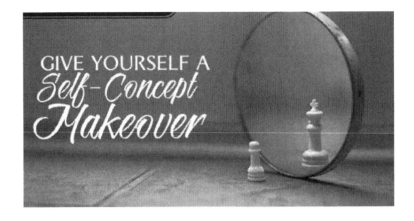

ARE YOU A VICTIM?

Consider it pure joy, my brothers and sisters, whenever you face trials of many kinds, because you know that the testing of your faith produces perseverance. Let perseverance finish its work so that you may be mature and complete, not lacking anything. James 1:2-4 (NIV)

Do you find yourself feeling that the world is against you and it's preventing you from living the life you want? Then let me be the first to give you the push you need to redirect yourself toward a more peaceful, existence. Understanding what it means to be a victim can be the first step toward drastically altering your life.

Our lifestyle choices are usually the culprits that prevent us from moving ahead. So, getting in touch with how we feel and why will clarify the reasons why authentic living is eluding us. The future will also benefit.

Childhood experiences and past mistakes can complicate your emotional life and trigger feelings of negativity and helplessness during your adult years.

Those feelings can eat away at the very foundation of your sense of self and incapacitate your ability to live in purpose. How you react or respond to challenging situations reveals a lot about the way you live your life. The good news is that you and God are the only ones who possess the power to alter your path in life. You can choose in this moment to make being a victim a thing of the past. You can survive whatever you've been through. Your latter can be better than your former.

Move from victim to victor.

"Refuse to become a victim of your circumstances and give a lift to your potentials each and every day against the wish of any obstacle you encounter!"

~ Israelmore Ayivor

AUTHENTIC MOMENT: Let me be the first to say, I did not have an awful childhood. My parents were awesome. Even though they were divorced, each of them did what they could to make me feel loved. However, they were human. There were times when being compared to others made me feel inadequate. Parents often believe that if they extol the positive characteristics of other children it will improve their child's outcomes. But, comparison does the opposite. Those who are compared to others have a diminished sense of individuality and ultimately come to believe they must behave and do what others do to receive acceptance. For a long time, I was no different.

Conformity was the norm. After all, I was a PK (preacher's kid). The belief was that if you follow the majority opinion you would be okay. You would belong, and you would be secure. Individualism, while not discouraged, it was also not encouraged. It can unwittingly be soul-destroying and kill the dreams of a potential Maya Angelou, Oprah Winfrey, or Terri McMillian. I learned to ignore what I wanted to do and instead tried to do what was expected. Didn't always turn out like I expected but I tried. It is generational because I wanted my children to be free thinkers but if they stepped too far out of the box (in my opinion or in what I perceived to be the opinion of my parents mostly) it made me uncomfortable.

What Does It Mean to Live Like a Victim?

According to the Wordbook Dictionary, a "victim" is described as someone who is "unfortunate" and who "suffers from adverse circumstances."

Consider the following points to determine if you might be living life as a victim:

1.   Your thoughts are affected. Negative thinking follows you everywhere you go

2.   You ask yourself "why" a lot. Why does everything in my life have to be so challenging? Why can't everyone just leave me alone? Why do others constantly make demands on me? Why doesn't anyone understand me?

3.   You lament. Rather than look for solutions and consider ways to change, you whine and complain, "Poor me! Wasting precious that could be better spent creating a life of purpose.

4.   Your feelings tell the tale. Do you walk around feeling like you're less important or not as smart as others? Feeling like you are damaged goods has probably crept into the dark corners of your mind. It's likely your self-esteem is low.

5. Anger and resentment have become comfortable for you. In fact, you experience these feelings on a regular basis.

41

‣ You resent it that your neighbor won $7,000 in the state lottery. She already has a nice car, great clothes, and a respectable job.

‣ as usual, the good stuff happens to others and the bad stuff happens to you.

6. You look around and feel jealous and envious of others. Most of us have experienced some type of jealously or envy at some point in our lives.

‣ perhaps, you've wished that you could live in that house across the street with its beautiful flower gardens and stunning entryway. It disappoints you to think that the Smiths get to pull into that driveway each day, walk through that lovely door, and live in the place you covet.

7. You blame yourself when things go differently than you hoped. When others mistreat you, something tells you that it's because of something you did or that's "just the way it is."

8. You blame others for challenging situations in your life. Everyone faces difficult situations. The challenge is to accept responsibility and avoid blaming others.

‣ Isn't it time to abandon the mindset that when others do Behavior A, you have no choice but to do Behavior B?

9. Feeling helpless is a way of life. Perhaps you tend to watch what goes on around you as if you're uninvolved. Things just happen. The world seems like a cold, unsupportive place. You may falsely believe you're unable to do anything that will change your situation or better your life.

If helplessness is the over-riding emotion in your life, it's likely that you feel like a victim. But your thoughts and feelings aren't the only signs.

"Over the years, I learned to smile or laugh when I was supposed to. I kept my true self hidden; I did not need to unleash my pain on the world around me. Instead, I taught

myself to ignore it. I did not realize that the pain was eating away at my soul." ~ J.D. Stroube

Actions or Inactions Speak Louder than Words

How do you behave at home and work? What about in relationships and social situations? Your behavior in various settings and situations often demonstrates to others how you feel about yourself. Does your behavior indicate that you've assumed the role of a victim?

Examine these actions to find out if you're living as a victim:

1.   At home, you waste time. As soon as you come in, you immediately go sit in your cushy chair. Even after dinner's done or when the weekend is here, you decide to ignore your home projects. You just don't feel like it. You'd rather be sitting on the sofa, watching television.

‣ The "hard days" you've had recently hold you back from creating the life you want. You have a valid excuse to do nothing, or so you think.

‣ The hours, days, months, and maybe even years fly by and you still haven't completed your painting project and other things on your "to do" list.

2. You avoid social situations. Meeting new people makes you sweat. Or you feel unsure about what to say when in a group. Others seem to look better, know just what to say, and live more fulfilling lives than you.

3. At work, you may stay in the background. You feel like nothing positive ever happens to you regarding your job. You believe that if you do the bare minimum, that's good enough.

‣ Is getting by and just collecting a paycheck your mantra?

4. You fade into the background when you're in social situations. The goal is to avoid being noticed.

You prefer to keep from becoming involved with others in any significant or meaningful way.

‣   For example, if you end up attending your office holiday party, you stake out one area where there's a co-worker you're comfortable with and stay there for the entire night.

5. In relationships, you avoid speaking up. Sharing real feelings scares you. You feel like what you say isn't important enough or you want to avoid making your partner feel hurt or angry. Going along to get along is your motto.

6. Even if you are physically or emotionally abused, you stay. When you're in a relationship, you remind yourself that you've been abused before and that others are rarely kind to you. So, why expect anything different now? The helplessness is your anchor in the relationship.

Your inactions, as well as your actions, signal how you feel about yourself. When you believe the world happens to you and that you're powerless, you're living a victim role.

"As we do at such times I turned on my automatic pilot and went through the motions of normalcy on the outside, so that I could concentrate all my powers on surviving the near-mortal wound inside."

~ Sonia Johnson

AUTHENTIC MOMENT: It is so easy to go into auto-pilot. You get so use to it that it feels natural until it's not. I choose not to dwell on bad circumstances, but, it doesn't mean they don't happen. My challenge was learning to acknowledge them for what they were and still be true to myself.

We all walk through difficult situations during our lives. Learning to trust God is a lifelong process, and essential to living an authentic life. As I walk I have gained wisdom and truths that could only be learned through meditating on God's Word and allowing His truth to be lived out through me. My experience may not be your, but I can be a voice that reminds you of God's love and faithfulness.

I can tell you for a fact that the natural response to every trial I have faced has been to resist it. But the truth is when they are ordained by God they work together for our good.

Learn to receive all God has for you. Learn how to use "what Satan meant for evil" as the very thing that God will use for your good and His glory. God never wastes one moment of our pain or our sorrows.

I have chosen to grow during hard situations. As a result, I have seen God do what only He can do in my life.

Sufferings from the Past

We all emerge from the cocoon of our pasts, and our sense of self formed from our early experiences. Those experiences anchor us! Our identities are attached to them.

If you're stuck in a victim role, you're likely suffering with memories of past experiences that were scary, hurtful, or negative. You've been marked in some way with a terrible, internal scar.

Examine these points to help you figure out whether you've been psychologically damaged by your early life:

1. Thoughts of past abuse haunt you. Your childhood might have been rough. Adults were physically or emotionally abusive to you. You frequently find yourself thinking about these circumstances.

2. You feel wronged by prior events. Even if your family members disagree with your interpretation of the events from your childhood, you still feel like you were damaged by your situation.

3. You often wish your past could've been different. You wish you had lived in the house with the white picket fence and two perfect parents. Or

that you could have been an only child like your best friend. Things just didn't go the way you wanted.

‣ There's also the "why" question: why did these things have to happen to you?

4. Faulty beliefs result. Because your past was so difficult, you might think that it's impossible to live a happy life. You believe you've been tainted, and see no possibility for living a joyful, stable existence.

‣ Those old tapes, filled with negativity, are playing repeatedly in your head: "You won't amount to anything," "I'm just destined to live this way," or I won't ever have the life I truly want."

‣ Driven by your leftover emotions from the troubling events, these messages repeating themselves in your head can make you feel exhausted and "heavy."

‣ Are you burdened by your old baggage from the past?

Historical experiences of neglect, abuse, and abandonment can lead you to develop an overall view of life that causes you to live as a victim. Your vulnerabilities may be exposed, and you might feel hopeless about the future. But it's time to get a grip on your life. But you can find the power to put yourself on a more hopeful path.

AUTHENTIC MOMENT: My first marriage was far from ideal. I was physically and mentally harmed in a way that made me create walls that at most times were impenetrable. I thank God for my husband of 25 years because he was willing to walk with me as I struggled to overcome the victim mentality. But, it wasn't easy. Often, I behaved in a manner that said "I'ma get you before you get me." So, in many instances the molehill became a mountain. I had to truly reflect on myself and why I behaved that way. Honesty with myself and looking at the fact that many of our issues had little to do with my husband

and more to do with me and my inability to deal with issues from my past were difficult to overcome. But, we made it through and I am stronger and wider now.

"It is important for people to know that no matter what lies in their past, they can overcome the dark side and press on to a brighter world."

~ Dave Pelzer

Changing Your Script from Victim to Victor

You can act and change things, so that you no longer hear those old tapes playing in your mind. It's up to you to initiate self-corrective measures, so you can alter your outlook on life and change your opinion of yourself and those around you.

Put these ideas into action today to begin to live like a survivor:

1.   Open your mind. You can change anything in your life if you choose to. Even by taking small steps, you can head down a different path.

2.   Find your confidence. You've made it this far. Reflect on positive things you've achieved. Listing them will help you become more self-assured.

‣   Isn't it time you acknowledge that you've made some decent choices along the way?

3.   Make the decision to show your confidence to others. Although that work project has stumped a couple of your co-workers, you know exactly what you'd do with it and how to tackle the troublesome parts. Step up and offer to help. Although showing some self-assurance can be scary, you can do it.

4.   Think positive. Refuse to allow the old tapes from the past to keep playing in your head. Replace them with something positive. Instead of, "I won't amount to anything because of my past," think, "I survived my past, so I can achieve anything I put my mind to."

‣   Create an image in your mind of you burning all those old, negative messages.

5. Finish. Regardless of what you're doing, make every effort to finish the task. Use your calendar and prove to yourself that you complete what you begin. Schedule time to finish jobs. You'll feel uplifted when you see that you finish what you start.

6. Take responsibility. Own your own life. No one can make you feel a certain way or carry out a behavior unless you consciously choose to go along with them.

‣ You can do whatever you want to do. Create a happy life for yourself one action at a time.

7. Avoid blaming others for how your life goes now. Maybe your parents lacked nurturing skills or were even abusive. But you're in charge now. You're an independent adult who can take steps to ensure you're safe. Make your own life choices.

8. Adopt a new mantra. Create a short, motivational sentence you can say to yourself that will help you become a survivor. Consider these

examples: "No excuses - I create the life I want," "I can do all things through Christ who strengthens me," or "I'm not just a conqueror, I'm more than a conqueror." Say your mantra to yourself several times throughout the day.

‣ Place the mantra in writing on your refrigerator and bathroom mirror. Pretend you're an artist: paint the words of your mantra and frame it for a special place in your living room, bedroom, or kitchen.

‣ Telling yourself you can do something builds up your energy, so you can accomplish it.

‣ You might find it helpful to adopt your own special "anthem." Choose an anthem by thinking of a song from the past that energizes you and reminds you that you can make it.

‣ Choose a song that speaks to you and carries an uplifting message you love to hear.

‣ The point of having a mantra or anthem is that whenever your thoughts start heading back toward a negative place, you can say or sing it to yourself and turn your thoughts around.

AUTHENTIC MOMENT: My mantras have always been about saying what God says about me. "I am fearfully and wonderfully made" "I can do all things through Christ who strengthens me." "I am more than a conqueror" "God can prepare a table before me in the presence of my enemies."

9. Remind yourself about what is and isn't in your control. It's helpful to realize that you're unable to control what others do, but you can control your emotional and behavioral reactions to them.

‣ Remember that 100% of the time, you have a options in life. Allow yourself some time to consider them whenever a tough situation develops.

10. Keep a journal. (I know, you will hear about journaling many times in this book) When you write

down your thoughts and feelings, it provides insight about what's driving you. Only then can you figure out how you can change your life. Journal daily at first to get comfortable and establish the habit of looking within yourself.

11. Share genuine feelings when it's appropriate. Recognize that someone who cares about you is interested in hearing about how you really feel.

‣ If you're unsure your partner wants to know how you truly feel, talk with them about it. Let them know that you plan to verbally share your feelings more often. Ask them to listen and make efforts to understand you better.

‣ You'll want to mention that you'll pay attention to their thoughts, feelings, and words, as well.

12. Ask those you trust for feedback. Inquire about what others have noticed about your emotions in the past. How do they see you? Listen carefully for any

clues to how you're coming across to others. Feedback from others can help you figure out how you can alter your path to one that's more positive and hopeful.

13. Tell yourself it's okay to experience some discomfort. When you leave a predictable or comfortable place, physically or emotionally, it can be scary and intimidating.

‣ Making changes takes some effort, but it will eventually be worth any initial discomfort.

14. Focus. When you stay centered on your options, choices, emotions, and behaviors, you'll find life gets much easier.

‣ When we remind ourselves to stay personally centered, we relieve ourselves of the need to control others, earn their permission, or seek their approval. Keep your focus where it counts. The power is within you!

15. Consider seeking professional help. Depending on your situation, you may have a lot of personal work to do. You have the options to work these things through on your own, attend support groups, find a therapy group, or locate a therapist or counselor to assist you.

‣ Sorting out the details of your life and determining how to make changes will help you live a more conscious, fulfilling existence.

Use these "tools" to help you build a stronger sense of self and discover your desired pathway in life. Commit to applying these techniques in your daily life and unleash the survivor that's inside of you.

"Being a survivor doesn't mean being strong - it's telling people when you need a meal or a ride, company, whatever. It's paying attention to heart wisdom, feelings, not living a role, but having a unique, authentic life, having something to contribute, finding time to love and laugh. All these things are qualities of survivors."

~ Bernie Siegel

Start seeking out inspiring stories and literature. Reading about how others persevered and rose above life's challenges can add fuel to your fire and turn you into a survivor.

There is so much incredible literature that can light the fires of energy, motivation, and passion in you. Go to your local or online library for inspirational works. You'll be amazed at how much you can find to help you.

"I'm a survivor - a living example of what people can go through and survive."

~ Elizabeth Taylor

You can live an authentic life. The power to throw off the victim persona is in your hands. Doing so will be an ongoing process that requires daily effort, especially at first. But the rewards will be great.

"Forgiveness has nothing to do with absolving a criminal of his crime. It has everything to do with relieving oneself of the burden of being a victim--letting go of the pain and transforming oneself from victim to survivor."

Can I Be Me?

   ~ C.R. Strahan

Sharing this journey with you is part of my life assignment, my higher purpose. My desire is to reach out and help as many people as possible to live their lives authentically in purpose and on purpose; intentional about the choices they make and the outcomes they receive.

I established the E320 Institute in order to help people deliver their best life. Reading this book is evidence of the fact that you'd like to become empowered to empower yourself. Now is the time for you to do just that. If you're looking for additional help and inspiration on living authentically I highly encourage you to check out my program at E320Institute.com. Just so you know, the people that I enjoy working with are purpose driven , like accountability, don't quit, follow instructions, take action, and do the work.

Cheryl Lacey Donovan

My brethren, count it all joy when ye fall into divers temptations; Knowing this, that the trying of your faith worketh patience. James 1:2-3

Painful situations are a part of life, (boy do I know it) your perception is what propels you to authenticity or the lack thereof. Holding onto painful memories and feelings eliminates your ability to move forward

Negative emotions such as fear and heartache can affect your body and mind, leading to dysfunctional relationships, depression, stress, and disease. So, emotional intelligence is key to releasing the negativity in your life.

This section of the book will help teach you how to let go of the past and live the authentic life you deserve. Since you're reading this, you've already demonstrated the courage to make the transition. So, let's go!

"A lot of people say they want to get out of pain, and I'm sure that's true, but they aren't willing to make healing a high priority.

They aren't willing to look inside to see the source of their pain in order to deal with it." ~Lindsey Wagner

Why We Hold on to Pain and Anger

Naturally you should feel angry and hurt if your partner rejects you but holding onto this feeling for years will make it impossible for you to move into a healthier relationship.

The loss of loved ones can make it difficult to move on but holding on to these feelings for years only prolongs your unhappiness.

Clinging to negative emotions is generally the result of or inability or unwillingness to face our responsibility or be accountable for the role we played in the situation.

What Negative Contracts Have You Made?

For example, let's consider the emotion of loneliness and its possible underlying cause.

Barbara Ann Brennan, in her bestselling book Light Emerging, writes about the negative contracts we make and how these affect various areas of our lives. She gives the example of Gary, a lonely little boy who tries to get the attention of his busy and weary mother by doing things for her or helping her whenever she's feeling down.

When he finds his behavior succeeds in getting her to notice him, he repeats this pattern (much like a dog would!). He believes that if he doesn't take care of his mother, he won't get her love. His childhood experience teaches him that love comes at a price.

As a result, when he becomes an adult, his relationships with women are unsuccessful due to his exaggerated care-taking, whether it's a lover, employee, or business partner. He finds himself being sucked dry and ends up avoiding relationships. His loneliness upsets him, but he probably doesn't know why his relationships with women don't work.

Gary must dig deep to uncover the negative contract he made with his mother and reverse it. He must be ready for initial difficulties before he can ease into the new and positive pattern.

The women in his life may not like his new attitude at all. They can no longer count on his unconditional support and affection. However, Gary's new attitude will eventually benefit everyone involved. While he will realize he deserves love and doesn't have to pay for it, the women will become more independent by looking after their own welfare.

Gary may need the help of a professional counselor to understand the underlying cause for his unhappiness and be able to move forward. Don't hesitate to find the right guidance if you can't determine a cause for a negative pattern of emotions in your life.

AUTHENTIC MOMENT:

Man is not disturbed by events, but by the view he takes of them. – Epictetus

MY NAME IS CHERYL AND I AM A RECOVERING HERO CHILD! As the "Hero" I had an unconscious need to be needed, appreciated and valued. On the outside it looked like a good thing, but it threatened to make me bitter because I often found myself overextended. The need has often been met when I say yes and overpromise what I can deliver in order to be liked, please other people, or avoid the perceived consequences of saying no.

The family hero is the so-called "perfect child". They are generally responsible, respectful, and successful in school and probably even well dressed. On the outside this child looks; capable, talented, conservative, serious, trustworthy, strong, superior, creative, busy, arrogant or angelic.

These children share a variety of characteristics:

1. They succeed – by hard work and diligence, they are good students, hard workers, and/or star athletes.

2. They are overly responsible. They understand about cause and effect and consequences and they make the 'right' choices most of the time.

3. They're the shining star of this family. They're the kid that other parents compare their children to as a role model.

4. They usually continue to succeed all through life.

5. They are work horses, getting more done than most other groups of people.

6. They always follow through, regardless of what is asked of them or what is going on in their life.

7. They have trouble having fun, although they don't know it, because they define many of their activities (volunteer, familial or community) as 'fun'.

8. They take care of others, with or without that person's permission.

Heroes value themselves for getting things done. They perceive themselves as high energy people who are organized and efficient. Those identifiers are true, but the Hero usually takes on too much and doesn't understand about down time and relaxing. This child has always been rewarded in one way or another for working hard.

Ironically, this is often the hardest role to break away from, because the rewards become intrinsic to the Hero's self-identification and self-worth.

It's no wonder they often end up married to alcoholics, drug addicts, etc. etc. Or they become the workaholic adult who claims he/she is doing all this for the family when in truth, it's driven from their self-concept and self-image.

When the role is encouraged at the expense of the individual problems occur. On the inside The Hero often feels; anxious, inadequate, terrified of failure, angry, sad, lonely, worthless, ashamed or numb.

It has been no easy task breaking away from this pattern. I still deal with many of the remnants to this day. But, I have learned a few valuable lessons along the way. First, it is necessary for me to give myself permission to make mistakes and not be "perfect" Easier said than done. Nevertheless, done it must be. I've also had to learn how to create opportunities for play. Real play where I block out the cares of the world and focus on enjoying me. Lastly, and this is probably the most difficult because I loathe conflict and confrontation, but I have learned at least in part the necessity of expressing my feelings and needs to others

You Could Have Negative Emotions If...

It's not difficult to determine if you're inundated with negativity. There are some very specific behaviors exhibited by those dealing with negativity in their lives. When these behaviors arise they can be great indicators that you need to forgive either yourself or someone else.

1. Avoiding family or friends

2. Believing that life doesn't hold good things for you in the future

3. Drinking too much alcohol or doing illicit drugs

4. Constantly thinking of a painful event

5. Indulging in addictive behavior

6. Having problems with mental health

7. Being unable to enjoy the present

8. Hearing people say you have a chip on your shoulder

9. Planning to take revenge or punish someone

10. Having angry outbursts

Expecting Too Much

The world is filled with great expectations. However, expecting too much can lead to disappointment and frustration. The better choice is to accept that no one is perfect and that the only thing that is constant is change. Mistakes are inevitable so when things don't work out according to plan, don't get upset and don't give up.

Furthermore, never depend on others for your happiness, you because disappointment will come whether it's intentional or not. Remember, you're responsible for your own joy and blaming others for your misery, won't bring you any closer to happiness! Instead, focus on what you are grateful for.

Worth is not determined by abilities or talents it is determined by your humanity.

Ask yourself the following questions:

What am I contributing to the world around me? If your purpose in life is to live only for yourself or if all you want to do is party and hoard your belongings, you'll likely feel hollow over time. Am I taking family and friends for granted? This is so easy to do and most of us are guilty of this offense on some level. When it comes to family, we think we can get away with being our worst selves because they'll understand and love us unconditionally. Therefore, people often struggle with family relationships. Am I causing emotional or physical hardship for others? Perhaps unwittingly, we cause heartache for others. Some examples are teenagers who scorn the wise advice of their parents, people who take pride in jilting their lovers, those who cheat on their spouses, and husbands who beat their wives.

Dealing with a Broken Relationship

Depression is not uncommon after a break up. It can be difficult to understand how people who once loved each other can become total strangers. Your world is turned upside down as you try to start all over in uncharted territory.

Until I became a realist my heart remained broken. I intentionally took a few steps back and started to take notice of my life and my surroundings. It became apparent that I now had a new freedom from anxiety that I hadn't enjoyed in a long time. My happiness no longer depended on the actions of someone else. How refreshing.

As I moved forward I leaned to release the rejection I had internalized because holding on to it caused me to feel like I would never find anyone to love again. That thought was depressing.

If you feel this way, remember that your worth is not measured by what someone thinks of you! You're an awesome, unique person in your own right and you don't require another person to validate your God-Given gifts and talents. The loss is theirs!

Moving on After Heartbreak

Write it all down. Pen your feelings in a journal or write your ex a letter that you'll never send. Writing is cathartic. Writing about your experiences, whether negative or positive, will make you feel lighter. You'll have a better idea of how to make your next relationship a success.

Look for a pattern in your relationships. Is there a certain type of person you always find yourself attracted to? Does that work for you? Why or why not?

Many women, for instance, find themselves attracted to "bad boys." This type of man could have criminal tendencies or be violent; he could be a drug addict or a playboy. If you tend to find bad boys attractive, you may want to discover the reason so you can eliminate it.

Clean the house. Get rid of your ex's things. As you clean, imagine that you're cleansing your heart of the anger and pain.

Rediscover your hobbies and favorite activities. Maybe you didn't have much time for these while in the relationship, but now you can return to them. Keep yourself busy with things you like to do. You needn't depend on anyone else for your enjoyment.

Start an exercise routine. Exercise releases "happy" hormones and will make you healthy and trim. If you feel your overweight problem played a major role in your partner's rejection, join an exercise program and lose some weight. Do this in a sensible way, choosing an exercise routine which suits your body and mentality.

Spend some time with your friends. Talking to them about your break up may help lighten the heaviness you feel. Ask them about their lives. Shift the focus from you to them. Chat with others online who have suffered heartbreak as well.

Forgive your ex. Or forgive yourself if you blame yourself for the breakup. Forgiveness is essential if you want to move on and cultivate healthy relationships. It's essential even if you just choose to remain single because resentment and anger are negative emotions that will eat into your slice of happiness.

AUTHENTIC MOMENT: Scripture reminds us to be thankful in all things. It took me a minute, but I finally found a way to be thankful for the relationship and grateful for the love that was shared. At the end of the day it was necessary for my self-development or it wouldn't have happened. The lessons learned were painful but priceless. I learned a lot because of that relationship and now I have moved on. Spiritually my path expanded to places I never knew existed. I used the time alone to focus on my spirit man. Most of us are too busy nurturing our physical selves to think of our eternal spiritual selves, but we are spiritual beings in physical bodies.

Finding the well of joy within me took some time but now that I have found it I don't for it in others. Doing gave me a new sense of purpose. I've been on a never-ending journey to understand my true being and to manifest it as much as possible by getting in touch with my inner self through prayer and the guidance of the Holy Spirit.

Natural Remedies to Help Control Depression and Negative Emotions

EXERCISE

Exercise releases endorphins which foster a feeling of well-being. In a 2001 study carried out by Duke University in North Carolina, it was found that exercise is a more effective treatment for depression than antidepressants. In addition, there are fewer relapses and a higher recovery rate. You also develop self-esteem and confidence because you're trimmer and healthier.

But how do you motivate yourself to exercise when you're feeling down?

Start by doing small things like taking the stairs or walking to the store down the street, instead of taking the car. Try gardening or take the dog out for a walk. Take the stairs. Try to exercise in natural surroundings as nature has a soothing effect on the mind.

Brisk walking for 30 minutes a day (3-4 times a week) cuts the risk of diabetes by 50 percent. Plus, it's not hard on your joints. It keeps osteoporosis and many diseases including Alzheimer's and Parkinson's at bay. You could try other types of aerobic exercise such as tap dancing, swimming, running, or cycling.

If you think you can't exercise alone, go to the gym. Sign up for a calming yoga class. Yoga, like Tai Chi, improves your core (lower back and abdominal muscles) which gives you a feeling of balance and control. The movements require control of both mind and body. This physical sense translates into emotional balance.

Those who think they have not time for bodily exercise will sooner or later have to find time for illness

- Edward Stanley

When you're in an emotional bind, remind yourself of the things in your life that are going well. Begin your day with feelings of gratitude and think of your blessings throughout the day. A blessing could be something as simple as birds singing in your garden at dawn, a loving child or loving pets.

This will help you gain perspective. Observe your thoughts and weed out those that are negative, replacing them with empowering ones.

With gratitude comes appreciation, which is the key for living honestly and completely in the moment, untroubled by what has gone before and what could come. The perfectly lived moment will give birth to the perfect future moment.

The unthankful heart...discovers no mercies; but let the thankful heart sweep through the day and, as the magnet finds the iron, so it will find, in every hour, some heavenly blessings! - Henry Ward Beecher

JOURNALING (I TOLD YOU WE'D TALK ABOUT IT A LOT)

Once you've identified your negative emotions, the next step is to express the emotion you're feeling in words. Write it down in your journal. Research shows that writing about your feelings strengthens your immune system by alleviating the emotion.

Pay attention to your symptoms and write them down too. Perhaps your body is telling you to stop being self- critical, or easily angered. Maybe it's telling you to seek healthy relationships.

Journaling can be a very effective tool in your arsenal against negative emotions. Give it a try today!

This book gives you many powerful strategies for letting go of your negative emotions. Find some techniques that resonate with you and act to put them into practice. Soon you'll enjoy a new serenity and passion for life as you break free from the limits of negative emotions and discover the joys of a life filled with positivity!

Letting Go and Moving Forward

Forgiving ourselves can be the most difficult thing to do. The regret from all the wasted time, the shame of allowing situations to continue, the guilt of placing ourselves in harms way keeps us from letting go. The healthier choice is reflecting on the experience and learning from it so that we can move forward, because

by refusing to forgive ourselves of our regrets, we remain trapped in the past.

The good news is that there are some simple strategies that can help you come to terms with the things that you have done in the past, learn from these missteps, and embrace a future that includes a fulfilling life.

Try these strategies to help you forgive yourself and move forward:

1. Be honest with yourself and others about your error and hold yourself accountable. Reflect on the

mistake that you're unable to get over. Clearly identify what you did or didn't do and own up to it instead of trying to justify your actions.

Being honest with yourself and stating where you went wrong is the first step to releasing the pain, guilt, and shame that you feel.

Examine the events and circumstances that led to your mistake and be honest about how you felt then and are feeling now.

Consider how your mistake impacted others in both a physical and emotional sense.

Talk about your slip-up with a close friend, relative, counselor, or religious leader that you trust. Seek their opinion, feedback, and guidance about the severity of your error. It's likely that they'll see your mistake in a more forgiving light than you do.

2. Try to remedy the situation and make amends. Consider what you could have done differently to prevent your misstep and develop a plan to act

differently if you face a similar situation in the future. This can help you forgive yourself.

- Who has been affected? How badly were you or others hurt? Take it all at face value and Take the time to consider the impact outside of what you initially see. It's sometimes easy to overlook the smaller impact when the greater one is overwhelming.

Even if it has been quite some time since the situation occurred, if the result of your blunder caused harm to others, consider offering an apology and asking for forgiveness. This action alone can be very healing for both you and the person that suffered harm as a result of your mistake.

If you're unable to make amends with those who were directly affected, consider doing good deeds and acts of kindness to show to yourself and others that you truly regret your actions.

If your poor decision resulted in a monetary loss, seek to make restitution.

Share your story with others so that they might be able to avoid making the same error.

3. Accept your human imperfections. Above all, be kind to yourself. Remind yourself that you're human. There's nobody on the face of the earth who goes through life without making mistakes. However, it's important to remember that this doesn't excuse what happened.

- While accepting your human imperfections, take the time to identify your shortcomings. Use the opportunity to work on aspects of yourself that you might want to improve. Perhaps you'd like to further develop certain character traits or strengthen your skills in particular areas.

- When apologizing to yourself and others, you can point out that everybody makes mistakes, but you've learned from yours and have every intention of not repeating it.

1.   Challenge yourself to do better. The crucial final step to self-forgiveness is challenging yourself to do better. In the previous step, you accepted your imperfections. Now it's time to work at fixing the things you can.

- Is it that you need to learn to be nicer to others? You can work on that through conscious effort or group therapy.

- Try not to repeat the same mistake. That's one of the easiest ways to backslide and end up at square one again.

- Ask your supportive friends and family to help you on your journey. Remember that no man is an island.

Making things right might not happen overnight. What's important is that you forgive yourself and commit to turning things around.

AUTHENTIC MOMENT: I had to forgive myself for not being perfect. Yep, that's right. As hard as I tried to always do the right thing, there were times when it just didn't happen the way I intended. So, I had to let myself off the hook for making the wrong choices and creating more problems than solutions. It happens, and I learned from it.

We're all full of so much potential. That potential sits unused when we focus on our missteps and setbacks. Like me you must rise-up! Come to terms with the fact that you have so much more to give to the world. Chip away at the negativity until all that's left is your renewed spirit.

Realize that you've grown and you're no longer the same person that made the original error. Continue to seek ways to help others and avoid actions that might lead to a similar lapse of judgment in the future.

All of us make mistakes, and sometimes they come with serious and grave consequences. Regardless of how serious our errors might have been, all of us deserve forgiveness. Seizing the opportunity to repent and make amends will help everyone involved heal and put it in the past.

5 Toxic Beliefs that Keep you from Living Authentically

So, a man thinketh so is he. What you believe about you can either make you or break you. Rid yourself of the toxic beliefs that limit your life:

1.   It's too late, or I'm too old. There may be some things that are more difficult to accomplish at a certain age. But the number of things you can do is far greater than the number of things you can't.

- Abraham left his family behind at the age of 75 and went to place he knew nothing about with no road map of any kind. He became the father of a nation.

- Abraham and Sarah had a child well into their 90's

2.   Failure is bad. Failure is normal. If you're living, you're also failing from time to time. The trick is to fail in the right way and make good use of it. Failure is nothing more than an undesired result.

Take the opportunity to learn from your failures and adjust your approach. *If one way doesn't work, try another.*

3.   The past equals the future. You have an amazing ability to change and adapt. The past only affects you if you permit it. *You can choose to drop the past* and live in the present.

4.   People will criticize me, laugh at me, or think little of me. You're right. They will. They talked about Jesus and all He did was help others. No matter what you do, there are people that won't like it. And there's always someone ready to make a negative comment. Why do you care?

5.   I'm not smart, good with money, good with people, educated enough, special, or *fill in the blank.* No one is good at everything. You can learn to do what you need to do or surround yourself with people who make up for your lack of knowledge or ability

AUTHENTIC MOMENT: I knew for years that there was a Word in my belly, but I didn't want to share it because I was afraid that there would be backlash because I was a woman. I did everything I could not to use the word preach. I also served in every capacity I could other than preacher. I sang, taught Sunday School, wrote books, you name it. I came up with every excuse I could think of. It didn't help, I eventually had to give in to what I knew to be true.

A toxic belief could be holding you back from the life you deserve. These negative beliefs are difficult to recognize because you've been carrying them around for so long. Do a personal inventory and evaluate all the beliefs that inhibit you. How do you know they're true? What are they costing you? Get rid of them and proceed to bring your dreams to life!

BEND DON'T BREAK

Other people can easily become an excuse to give up the control you need in your life. Other people get in the way. Other people make demands on their time, so they can't achieve the things that they want to accomplish. Other people are responsible for the fact that they can't get their lives organized and really take the reins. Excuses, excuses, excuses.

People may challenge your ability to live authentically but accommodating others while having healthy relationships versus bending over backwards to be a people pleaser are two different things. People who live authentically don't do it by ingratiating others. They do it by setting boundaries and maintaining them.

This doesn't necessarily mean putting other people on the back burner because we are after all are social animals, and we survive and thrive in communities where we help each other to evolve and learn. However, we must be careful because if people who rely on us find that we are willing to compromise ourselves for them, they will put us to work until we reach our limits.

The tendency to want to make everybody around us happy, isn't unusual but sometimes by doing so we put our own happiness on the line. It is impossible to please everybody around us, so, the person who wants to focus on living authentically should take this as a lesson.

Focusing on our own needs is not selfish. It is quite the opposite. When you are in an airplane that is crashing out of the sky, you are more likely to be able to help your elderly seat-mate if you know to put your own oxygen mask on first. When we don't wear the oxygen mask, we can't effectively help those around us, because we haven't taken care of ourselves first.

This is a lesson that people-pleasers should keep in mind. If we don't take care of ourselves, we can't take care of others and it can become dangerous in the long run when we find ourselves worn out, overwhelmed, and tied down with the weight of other people's problems and expectations. The result is an identity crisis because we're so wrapped up in them that we no longer know who we are.

AUTHENTIC MOMENT: It is definitely not easy to raise children. Even when you think you're doing the right thing their perception can be totally different. I've learned this the hard was as I have gotten older. I now understand what it means when the elders say they go from being on your knee to being on your heart.

My identity for a long time was wrapped up in my children. Especially the youngest. I was giving so much of me to uplift him that I became lost in the struggle. It took the nudging of the Holy Spirit to help me begin to let it go. Literally, I heard the Spirit say, "you have to stop trying to be His God. How will he ever trust the creator if you always step in?"

As usual I was so caught up in making things right that I lost sight of reality. I wanted to be a faithful steward of the charge of motherhood, but that charge had long since changed from parenting to mentoring but I didn't get or rather refused to read the memo.

The key to living authentically is in being able to let yourself have the freedom you need to say no. You can still be part of the social scene. But the trick is in being able to set healthy boundaries so that you don't end up feeling as if you are being taken advantage of.

Like the mighty reed, we need to bend, compromising only what truly needs to be compromised. We cannot break ourselves by taking on too much weight at once. Anybody who can step on us to serve themselves is likely to do just that. What we need to do is learn how to set healthy boundaries. And the first step in doing so is to put the oxygen mask on yourself and identify where in your life you could be more assertive.

Balancing family and domestic matters can often be a difficult and messy task. In this case, it is best to sit down and have a mature and respectful conversation with your family members about your expectations and about what is reasonable to expect from you considering your responsibilities. Once a system is in place, it is much easier to assert yourself.

Assertiveness is intimidating, but it is the most rewarding thing that you can do for yourself. Being assertive requires a firm understanding of your own boundaries and limitations. Make sure that you think carefully about what it is you are willing to do, and what is too much for you. Be willing to be honest with those around you and stay firm when you tell them no. People respect a person with boundaries.

Goal: *Sit down and write a list of things that you feel you do out of a people-pleasing habit. Address each of these ways with assertive but calm ways that you can respond to these situations and set a healthy boundary for yourself. For example, if you feel that a co-worker takes advantage of the way you pick up the slack for them, simply stop picking up the slack and let them know that you do not appreciate what they are doing. Practice communicating calmly and clearly without being accusatory, such as using "I" statements, so that others will be willing to accept your no* *for what it is and are less likely to perceive it as a personal attack.*

Cheryl Lacey Donovan

NOTES

Stop Seeking Approval from Others

Where did the need for approval begin? No one really knows. However, approval-seeking behavior is self-sabotaging. Trying to impress others is exhausting and minimizes your own importance and individuality.

AUTHENTIC MOMENT: I've already told you I'm the hero child. Seeking the approval of others was part of my obsession for much of my life. Dependent on approval—so dependent that I bartered away all my time, energy, and personal preferences to get it—divorced me from my true self. It's no wonder that rage at times wasn't far behind. Pleasing others is like an addiction: When we do it because we really want to, it's a wonderfully life-affirming way to strengthen a relationship, but when it's motivated by obligation and powerlessness, it can become degrading. I have found that the key to an authentic emotional life, is to follow your true heartfelt desires. Free yourself from the need to receive approval from others:

1.   Give your opinion freely. One symptom of approval-seeking tendencies is the hesitance to share your opinion. You might say something that the other person doesn't approve of. And since it was your opinion, they might not approve of you either. Give your opinion, even if it makes you uncomfortable.

2.   Avoid judging others. If you're overly critical of others, it's only natural that you assume others are the same towards you. By avoiding this type of behavior in yourself, you'll drop the assumption that everyone else is judging you. Allow others to be as they are. It makes life more interesting. Enjoy the differences.

3.   Realize that disapproval can be used as a weapon. Many people use disapproval as a means of getting what they want. They may disapprove of you to enjoy the fruits of your submission.

- Call people on their disapproval of you. Ask them to explain themselves. *Remember that most negative people are looking for a victim, not a fight.* When you stick up for yourself, many of the bullies disappear.

4.   Be aware of what happens when someone disapproves of you. *Nothing.* We seem to be born with an intense desire to fit in. But what actually happens when someone disapproves of you?

5.   Do some things for yourself. Show yourself that you're important by focusing some of your time and energy on yourself.

- Fill your life with things that are important. Volunteer with an organization that's doing important work. Write a book that you believe will change lives for the better. Find ways to spend your time on things you consider to be important.

Being overly concerned about the opinions of others is damaging to your self-esteem. *Each time you seek approval, you're diminishing your own importance.* You're causing yourself pain. Allow your individuality to be seen and experienced by others.

Can I Be Me?

NOTES

How Feeling and Looking Your Best Can Help You Live Authentically

The American Psychological Association says, "Studies have shown that women who exercise regularly, eat right, get sufficient sleep and find satisfaction in their work and personal lives have LESS Depression, Anxiety and illnesses, such as heart disease."

Self-care is an afterthought for most women.

According to the US Department of Labor,

• 70% of mothers with children under 18 works, and more than 75% are employed full-time

• Today, mothers are either the primary or only earners for 40% of households that have kids under age 18 compared with 11% in 1960

Statistics Brain reports that...

- 86% of working mothers say they are "sometime/frequently" feel stressed

- 40% of working mothers say they "always feel rushed"

Suffering from physical, mental, and emotional burn out is inevitable as we slowly deplete our resource and become bankrupt. Stress and exhaustion abound as our cup empties and we find that we have nothing left to give to anyone including ourselves. But who has the time for self-care? We're busy taking care of kids, husbands, work, you name it.

AUTHENTIC MOMENT: I have been in the medical field for many years. Anxiety attacks were something I had heard of before but had never experienced. Imagine the first time I experienced one. I thought I was having a heart attack. Exhaustion, burnout, and mental fog it all caved in on me like a mountain full of rocks. That was the first time I recognized how far from "me" I had come. I found myself being resentful, angry and incapable of not only enjoying my life, but getting anything done.

Self-Care 101

Self-Care Is…

Taking personal responsibility for one's own physical, emotional, mental and spiritual health. It is good for your mind, body, spirit, life, and soul. It is NOT selfish. It is a habit that makes you flourish, not just function. It is a choice. It is preventive, imperative, and a deliberate effort. It is about making yourself a priority. Self-care is a lifelong practice. It is empowering; a lifestyle and a ritual.

When we ignore our needs and don't take care of ourselves it can lead to come serious consequences including physical, emotional, spiritual, and quality of life difficulties. Let's look at a few of the issues that can result from the lack of self-care.

Physical

Stress, a critical component in major disease processes like heart disease, stroke and obesity, is also a major consequence of a lack of self-care.

As the stress hormone cortisol surges through the body it causes serious complications, including reduced immunity, deteriorating organ function and accelerated aging of both the mind and body.

According to Stress.org, 3 out of 4 doctor office visits are stress related and stress is the basic cause of 60% of all human illness and disease.

Stress increases risk of heart disease by 40%, risk of heart attack by 25% and risk of stroke by 50%.

Hectic lifestyles that lack some type of self-care component also result in unhealthy diets and lack of exercise that further increase risks for chronic health problems, one of which is type 2 diabetes, which is at epidemic levels in the United States.

According to the Mayo Clinic, stressed out women are more likely to suffer from chronic fatigue syndrome and thyroid disorders, both of which are believed by experts to be caused at least in part by hectic health-compromising lifestyles.

Emotional

Exhaustion, anger, bitterness, and anxiety are all outcomes of a lack of self-care that lead to resentment. These feelings spill over into personal relationships.

Mental

Depression, anxiety and other mental health problems can also be attributed to a lack of self-care. In fact, women suffer from depression at a four times higher rate than men. Burnout, overwhelm and brain fog are some of the disastrous consequences of a hectic lifestyle that does not address self-care.

One study (Life Event, Stress and Illness, Mohd. Razali Salleh) states, "The correlation between stressful life events and psychiatric illness is stronger than the correlation with medical or physical illness. The relationship of stress with psychiatric illness is strongest in neuroses, which is followed by depression and schizophrenia."

Spirit

Often overlooked our spirits suffer profoundly from a lack of self-care. Anna Quindlen summarizes this consequence well in her book, Being Perfect, "Someday, sometime, you will be sitting somewhere.... And something bad will have happened: You will have lost someone you loved or failed at something at which you badly wanted to succeed. And sitting there, you will fall into the center of yourself. You will look for some core to sustain you. And if you have been perfect all your life and have managed to meet all the expectations of your family, your friends, your community, and your society, chances are excellent that there will be a black hole where that core ought to be."

Cheryl Lacey Donovan

NOTES

So, we've looked at what self-care is as well as the consequences of the lack thereof. But now let's look at the reality that self-care is often easier said than done. Roadblocks to self-care do exist. I've listed a few of them here.

Women Are Nurturers to Everyone but Themselves

We dedicate our energy and find time where there is none to help our kids, friends, bosses, and family but we can never seem to find time for our own needs.

Everything else ranks higher. Everyone and everything else that is constantly bombarding us with big things to worry about takes precedence over our own fundamental needs for critical 6things like calm, quiet, rest, and even fun.

Somehow, there is always something that is more important. So, we push our own self-care needs down the list, until eventually they are no longer on the list at all.

Women are taught to care for others as making sacrifices is entangled with being a mother and a wife. Guilt sets in when we say no. We also worry that we are being selfish when we take time for ourselves or say no to someone's request.

Acknowledge these facts and understand that they are not the reality but are rather perceptions of our own making. Taking time for yourself is not only beneficial, it is imperative because it will help us take better care of ourselves so that we can be there whole and repaired for our loved ones.

Not Asking for Help – Doing It All Yourself

I must concede that I am like a lot of women when it comes to asking for help. I am often driven to do everything by myself because somehow like many women I don't want to appear weak.

Then there's the moment where it all becomes too much and I'm desperate to ask for help but too afraid to do so.

Have you ever found yourself in a position that you fought to get, so you insisted on doing everything yourself? Even though you weren't entirely sure of the full expectations you didn't want to speak up to clarify or ask for support, you thought you'd figure it out on your own and even though you did, it was frustrating and difficult to get there. It's something that has happened to all of us at some point, yet we don't learn the lesson as quickly as we should.

Here's what happens when you insist on doing it all yourself and refuse to just ask for help.

The Alienation of Others

One of the biggest aspects of not asking for help is a failure to communicate your struggles with the people around you, whether it's at home or in a work situation. By refusing to ask for help, it makes it more difficult for other people to reach out to you.

Alienating others in turn alienates you.

Self-Care out the Window

One of the biggest issues with not requesting help when you need it is that it shows disrespect to you. You're disrespecting your self-care by taking on more than you can handle. You don't have to say yes to absolutely everything, nor must you struggle along with everything that is on your plate now. Speak up!

Tips for Asking for Help

Why have you been afraid to ask for help in the past? Was it because you were afraid of appearing weak or incapable? Well, the truth is the opposite; there is strength in asking for help.

The key is in asking the right way:

- Don't wait until the last minute

- Ask the right person

- Don't make them feel like they have no choice

- Be clear about what you need

- Ask them face to face and follow it up in an email

- Thank them

- If you can, help others when they need it

AUTHENTIC MOMENT: My mindset has always been not to be a burden to someone else. If there is an assignment for me to do or if there is a responsibility that is mine (i.e., children) then I felt obligated to do it myself. No one owes me anything. If I accepted the challenge or created the task, then I should be able to handle it.

Lack of Self-Awareness

Does this sound familiar? You're having a conversation with someone and out of nowhere you become extremely frustrated and begin screaming at the person you're talking to about something that is insignificant. Or maybe you find yourself too exhausted to lift your head off the pillow. Don't fell alone. This is usually when most women realize that they have completely neglected taking care of themselves.

Notice how you feel throughout the day. Are you run down? Tired? Can't think straight? Eating a lot of carbs and sugar filled junk? These are all signs that you are not centered, overly stressed, and headed towards major burnout.

Self-awareness is the ability to identify, recognize, and understand that is really going inside yourself.

Psychology professor Dan McAdams of Northwestern University explains that, "The stories we tell ourselves about our lives don't just shape our personalities — they are our personalities."

Rarely do we take the time to notice how we are feeling and doing in general on a day-to-day basis because we are running around without taking a minute to stop, check in with ourselves, and just be.

Consider spending time alone during the day to reflect and consider what your truest and deepest needs for health really are. Once this has been identified you can begin to plan how you will fulfill these needs.

Mindfulness is another great approach to gaining self-awareness. By becoming aware of the present moment, you can improve all your future ones.

Research (Richard Davidson) has found a direct correlation between changes in the brain and mindfulness, creating a sense of calm and wellbeing in study subjects and reducing anxiety and anger.

AUTHENTIC MOMENT Many of us spend a lot of time living in the past or planning for the future. Very seldom do we take the time to live in the moment.

It took some time for me to understand what living in the moment looks like. But I can tell you that it helps to create order in the chaos.

Now, I must be transparent. Everyone may not understand it in the beginning. Especially those people who have had uninterrupted access to you in the past. Nonetheless, if they love and respect you they will understand.

Example: When I am at work, my family knows that unless it is an emergency they should wait to connect with me during lunch or after I come home. Parenthetically, my job knows that once my normal work hours are up their access to me ends until the next day. This way I can be in the moment giving all my time to the tasks, people, and issues at hand.

When everyone has access all the time, it creates a hectic atmosphere that causes stress, burnout, and even resentment.

Learning to Say No

In her book, The Art of Extreme Self-Care, Cheryl Richardson explains the reasons we have a hard time saying no...

"We don't want to feel guilty.

We don't want to disappoint others because we know how bad it feels.

We don't have the language to let someone down with grace and love.

Our fear of conflict and our desire to keep the peace keep us from telling the truth.

We want people to like us and are uncomfortable when they don't."

Richardson further explains that to become healthy we must at times say no, and this means, "You must learn to manage the anxiety that arises when other people are disappointed, angry, or hurt. And they will be. When you decide to break your pattern of self-sacrifice and deprivation, you'll need to start saying no, setting limits, and putting boundaries in place to protect your time, energy, and emotional needs."

Easier said than done, this is a change that is necessary. It will help you avoid the overload that occurs because of never saying no especially, when saying yes will have a negative effect. For some of us, it never even occurs to say no, we just agree to any request, and then when we realize what a hardship it is, or that we really are overextended we feel regret, anxiety, resentment and maybe even some guilt at letting our own selves down.

Worse yet, is when we are okay with sacrificing our needs to help someone else. This habit is self-destructive as it slowly eats away at our own reserves.

AUTHENTIC MOMENT Can you say double booked and overwhelmed? Yes, that has happened to me on many occasions. Not intentionally mind you, but it happened nonetheless.

One of the things I had to learn to do was to stop agreeing to things on the spot. Instead I've learned to let the person know that I need to make sure that I'm not otherwise engaged and then I take the time to consider my answer carefully and get back to them.

Remember that we are not responsible for other people's reactions, we are only responsible for ourselves, so while some may get upset and try to make you feel guilty, let it go and keep yourself in mind first.

The truth is that those people who cannot respect your boundaries are not real friends and doing things out of guilt is not the foundation for a healthy relationship. Your real friends and loved ones will understand because they care about you and not what they can get from you.

Busyness

Have you ever found yourself so entirely consumed by the activities in your daily life that you forgot to look after what should be your priority (you)? Being "too busy" is yet another major roadblock to self-care.

How intentional are you about making sure you are taken care each day? Do you often forget to eat lunch, or make a variety of different meals every night just to cater to everyone else's tastes?

Busy truly is a disease because you get so caught up with your to do list you neglect yourself.

Essentially, you are that pot of rice that you've shifted to the back burner while focusing on the rest of dinner. Even though there is nothing worse than bad rice and it plays a major role in the meal, you forget all about it. Much like you forget about yourself in your race to take care of everything and everyone else.

Much of the time, we live our lives going from one task to the next, often putting ourselves and our health on the bottom of our list of priorities. This may seem convenient at the time, but in the long run we notice all of the ways that neglecting ourselves has actually harmed us.

Instead of allowing other situations and people to take priority over your time, make sure that you are putting yourself and your body first. When you are meeting your own fundamental needs, then you place yourself in a better position to help others.

When we spend too much time in our heads rather than nurturing a mind and body connection, it can become very overwhelming, whether we consciously realize it or not. Our minds become accustomed to ignoring our needs to the point that we experience burnout without even being able to pinpoint just what it is that we are burnt out from!

Not only that, but sometimes it can be so easy to just let ourselves go physically, and before we know it we are suffering from health problems and body issues. We don't realize just how important it is to make an investment of time in our health!

Health and success may seem like they are not necessarily connected, and the truth is that maybe they shouldn't be. But unfortunately, there *is* a connection, and it is a rather significant one! When we are not tending to our health and fitness, our mind and concentration tend to suffer. When our brains aren't capable of operating at peak capacity, we not only miss opportunities that might help us to be successful, but we find ourselves wasting time by doing silly, unproductive things, such as zoning out or nurturing lazy and unhelpful habits.

Fitness and exercise are things that many people struggle with, especially in a world like modern day North America. We are given flashy screens and conveniences, but that doesn't mean that we should let ourselves give in to the temptations of lazy 21st century living. Truthfully, twenty minutes out of every day to focus on your health and exercise is all it really takes to ensure that you are on the path to the best you possible!

One thing that can help a lot is having a steady morning routine that gets you really primed for the day ahead. There is nothing more refreshing than waking up, and, after brushing your teeth and drinking a glass of lemon water a tablespoon of apple cider vinegar, stretching and exercising in front of an open window. Our bodies become acclimated to these types of routines and rejoice in being exposed to fresh air and healthy movement. It is easier to make time in the beginning of your day than it might be to try to squeeze something in later, knowing that your schedule can become unpredictable and chaotic the further in you get.

Try to remember that your personal success is directly related to how strong your mind and body connection is. Exercising three times a week can significantly improve your outlook! There is science behind it, so try to make sure that you are doing what you can to stay focused on your physical fitness. Your brain and your body will thank you!

Goal: *Wake up every morning and set aside time for yourself to stretch and "salute the sun" so to speak. Use this time to focus your energies on yourself and your own physical well-being. Write out a plan to exercise at least three times per week, doing things that you enjoy and that serve your body. Make sure that you are being kind to yourself and easy on your body, only pushing yourself to a degree that is healthy and not destructive. Exercising just three times a week can improve your blood flow and increase your ability to focus and create, ultimately providing you with a great tool in mastering your destiny.*

NOTES

No Excuse Zone

What is your excuse for not taking care of yourself? All of us like to believe that we are always doing the best that we can but the reality is if we are overwhelmed and tired it can become very easy to make excuses for why we don't care for ourselves. Our obligations and responsibilities toward our societal roles and family roles may seem like all we have time for. Wasted hours doing nothing occur when we are down on ourselves about what we can reasonably expect to accomplish. Part of this might be a lack of self-confidence, which can be addressed using the tools in this book. However, some of this tendency may be a fear of success. So afraid, that we might do things that will cause us to get in our own ways.

This might seem absurd, but have you ever felt a surge of fear when you realized you were good at something r when you were recognized for something you did well? This fear arises out of your perception that to whom much is given much is required. That's right you will be held responsible. The truth is that we are aware that when we perform well at something, it puts pressure on us to continue to succeed, and other people begin to expect a certain level of performance.

However, we must be willing to face our fears head on and stop trying to convince ourselves that we are not capable of achieving our dreams. Sure, maybe it is easier not to attempt it because then we can live our lives without being faced with a long road of trial and error and responsibility. But we cannot continue to make excuses not to succeed. Finding reasons why it just isn't possible to work toward our true passions only limits our abilities when we allow those excuses to dictate our lives and convince us that we will never be good enough.

The truth is that each one of us has a higher potential that we can aspire to; a higher potential that deserves to be explored and nurtured, not shut down by the excuses we make to ourselves so that we don't have to deal with the responsibilities of success.

If you are tired of getting in your own way, or of compromising for other people rather than moving forward and focusing on your own passions, then it is important for you to come up with a plan of action. What are you going to do to stop yourself from making excuses that allow you to fail without taking any personal responsibility for it? What are you going to do to stop compromising your vision for the expectations of others?

Here are a few ideas. First, begin to really examine yourself and your thoughts. Learn to recognize when you are cutting yourself too much slack and letting yourself off the hook. The only way to truly become a master of your own destiny is to allow yourself to take responsibility for your future. If you fail, you have only yourself to blame. And that sort of blame really doesn't feel good. When you look back on your life and find that you constantly made excuses not to achieve the things you truly care about, you will see that there were choices that you could have made to better your situation. You didn't have to put others first at all times. You could have made time for yourself.

Instead of living a long life of regrets and living with a lack of fulfillment, take responsibility for yourself in the here and now. Practice mindfulness techniques that will provide you with a realistic interpretation of the events going on in your life. Take responsibility for every minute in your day and decide what is truly worth spending those extra moments on.

Sure, you have responsibilities and obligations, whether to your job or to your family, and those can be important. But you are important too. And it is extra important to stop making excuses that allow you to let your life pass by before your eyes without you feeling the urgent need to step in and direct those minutes toward achieving your dreams!

Goal: *Journal about all the self-defeating thoughts that you have during the day and come up with affirmations to counter those thoughts. If you find yourself thinking something like, "I'm not smart enough to figure that out and succeed at my dream job," counter that thought with an affirmation such as "I am smart and capable, and I can achieve anything I set my mind to." Do the same when you find yourself making excuses to take the easy way out. The easy road is not necessarily the right road to travel. If you want to master your destiny, make sure that you are taking care of your biggest obstacles, even if that includes yourself!*

Cheryl Lacey Donovan

Can I Be Me?

NOTES

Walking on Water

Sometimes it seems like the longer we spend daydreaming about our goals, the more out of reach they become. It can be defeating to realize that what we want to do is going to require tremendous efforts on our part, and that effort may seem out of our league. These types of realizations can leave us feeling defeated and unmotivated, even before we have taken the first step in trying!

Defeatist attitudes are the fastest way to destroy our own happiness. Sure, dreaming big is often discouraged because big dreams require a lot of work and a lot of resources, but that doesn't mean that we can't accomplish great things, even as a team of one person! What it means is that we must look outside of ourselves - beyond our brainwashed minds telling us that all we have in life are limitations and realize that when we break the glass ceiling over our heads that keeps us trapped in our own discouragement, anything is possible!

However, for us to make any headway in achieving our goals, we must do so with a practical and measured approach. We hear all the time about the rare genius who was able to take an idea and turn it into a wildly successful reality. We often view these people with awe and disbelief; as if they are larger than life and it is somehow a fluke or a strange event that had contributed to their success. We are all impressed by people who can go out there and achieve the goals that they set for themselves.

But what most of these people will tell you is that there is nothing all that special about them. The reason they were able to accomplish their goals had less to do with opportunities and connections and networking, and everything to do with their own ability to plan and see things through to the end.

Their goals were achieved because they had the secret to walking on water figured out. They knew how to break their goals down and work on them, bit by bit, until they were accomplished.

And that's exactly what you must do too. It isn't impossible to achieve your dreams. In fact, all it takes is some serious planning. Start out with looking at your end goal. Visualize it and write it out in detail so that you know exactly what it is that you are aiming for.

Go backwards from there. For example, if your dream is to have a successful business, what is it that you must do to get there? Well, for a business to be successful, you will need good clients. To have good clients, you will need a product and a service that they can trust. To do that, you need to hire a good team that gets the job done and have a product that people are willing to pay for. For that type of product, you need to first get a patent on said product and have it developed and tested out first. To do that, you need to research patents and brainstorm ideas for the types of products you would be interested in providing to consumers. And no matter where you are in the stages of your life and in developing your business model, you can put a few hours aside per week to go toward research!

Start with the small aspects of your big plan and keep knocking them out of the park one by one. Break the goal down into small, easy to digest pieces that are easier for you to understand and work toward accomplishing. This is truly the key to being able to walk on water and achieve things that other people might think that it is impossible for you to do. Everybody wants to be able to do great things in life, but without understanding the nature of achieving goals and how to get from point A to point B, there is almost no point in even considering such goals.

You must be willing to put the work and dedication into making sure that you have a blueprint to success all laid out and ready to go. Don't stress yourself out worrying about the big picture and feeling overwhelmed by the huge dream you want to reach. Instead, break that huge dream down into smaller dreams that ultimately come together to form the big picture. That is a simple and sure-fire way to getting your goals accomplished and turning your dreams into a reality!

Goal: *Instead of being overwhelmed by the amount of work needed to put into achieving a dream that looks too good to be true, try buying a notebook and writing down your goal. Think backwards about the steps that you must take to achieve that goal and break the big ideal down into smaller goals that can be achieved over time. If you don't want to go backward, that's fine, you can also try to do it from the bottom up. Just do your best to make sure that you have the insight necessary to make the planning process a* *success. No matter how difficult it may seem to achieve your goals, it is nothing compared to the negativity we place on our own shoulders when we convince ourselves that what we want to accomplish is impossible, and too big for one single person to do on their own! That's not true. You can walk on water and create the reality of your choosing, simply by learning how to plan and break your goals down into manageable chunks!*

Cheryl Lacey Donovan

NOTES

Detoxing Your Relationships

Blessed is the man that walketh not in the counsel of the ungodly, nor standeth in the way of sinners, nor sitteth in the seat of the scornful. Psalms 1:1

No matter where you are at in life, whether you are already a successful person in your chosen field or if you are simply struggling to get your goals figured out, toxic people and situations are everywhere. When we are unable to identify these toxic people and behaviors, it can be a huge issue, one that is extremely detrimental not only to our well-being, but to our future as well.

Toxic people do not want to see you succeed. They want to bring you down to their level and convince you that you are incapable of doing the things that you set out to do. They are so mired in negativity that the only way they think that they will be able to survive is to spread that negativity to others. This gives them temporary relief from their own miserable lives, but it is never enough to make them truly happy. What they will do instead is come back and keep picking at you until they are satisfied that you will never accomplish anything good.

They do not want to believe that anything positive can happen, either to themselves or to others. They do not want to see other people happy because it makes them bitter. They will often be manipulative people who are out to further their own agendas and work themselves into positions of power over others, because most toxic people see the world in terms of power and control. They have a hard time getting along with others because they have a shallow ability for empathy.

These people can show up anywhere, and it is especially harmful if they are people that you already know and trust. It may take years to identify toxic behaviors in the people that you care about, but once you do and you are given a break from their influence, you may find yourself feeling better than you have in years.

Toxic people and behaviors are dangerous to our mental health and well-being. They make us doubt ourselves and put our self-worth into question over sometimes ridiculous things. It is hard for them to communicate in a healthy way and we may find ourselves being blamed for their mistakes or being made to feel responsible for their emotional lives when in truth, only they are responsible for themselves and that is the way it will always remain, no matter how bitter they may be.

The reason toxic people are an issue when it comes to becoming the master of your own destiny is because toxic people often like to meddle where they don't belong. If they see that you are trying to make your life better, they will bring you down. If they see that you are capable of things that they don't think they themselves are capable of, they will belittle your achievements and talents to make themselves feel better and to prevent you from succeeding. If a toxic person is threatened by you in any way, then they will do whatever it takes to help themselves feel better again.

This can mean disaster to a person who is sensitive to the criticism of others, or who does not know how to identify toxic behaviors in other people and instead trusts those around them to be constructive and helpful and honest.

If you can identify any indication of toxic behaviors in someone else, avoid them. These are not people who will help you on your way to becoming the master of your destiny. They simply can't, because *they* want to be the master of your destiny. You are better off without them.

Goal: *Become very familiar with toxic behaviors and learn how to identify toxic and manipulative people in your life. There are many resources that can help you to do so, and the more you know about these types of behaviors the better prepared you will be in the future when confronted with situations you may find yourself in with toxic characters. Journal about toxic behaviors you have seen and witnessed both in your own life and in movies or books. Also think honestly and critically about ways that you might also be toxic and behave in ways that are unhealthy toward other people as you attempt to accomplish your goals. Introspection can be difficult, but if you identify your negative behaviors and address them, then you are a true superhero. Once you have identified toxic behaviors in others, you can try to set firm boundaries with these people.*

If the boundaries you set are violated, it may be time to say good bye to the toxic person in your life once and for all.

Can I Be Me?

NOTES

Who Ya Wit?

As with anything, a good support network is everything. When it comes to empowering your life, it can be so difficult to find the resources that you need. The key that many successful people aren't telling you is that they became successful because they surrounded themselves with other successful people.

Humans are social animals. We are constantly taking cues from the people around us about how to behave. If we are surrounded by caring and generous people, we become more caring and generous ourselves, whether subconsciously or consciously. When we are surrounded by negative, defeatist people all the time, then we start to become more negative and defeatist ourselves. This can have a huge impact on whether we are priming ourselves for success. When we're not priming ourselves for success, we are priming ourselves for failure. It is that simple.

You should always think about the types of energy that your peer group is subjecting you to. If they are a positive group, then you are going to be more prone to having positive thoughts and interactions, whether you are interacting with that group or not. If they are negative, you can expect that you will begin to act and feel more negatively as time wears on.

It is extremely important to ensure that you are giving yourself the chance to interact with other successful people. When you surround yourself with people who are displaying the characteristics that you want to have yourself, it becomes easier for you to develop those characteristics simply by spending time with those people. They rub off on you in a most wonderful way, priming you to succeed in the ways you hope to succeed simply by being achievers.

Of course, it's not the only thing you have to do to be a successful person, and it also helps to have a support network of friends and family that are completely supportive of you and who you can hold yourself accountable to. When you are talking to people about your plans and they are asking questions about how you are doing and how things are coming along, you become more motivated to get to work and make sure that you are not letting them down.

Having people that hold us accountable to achieving our goals may seem cringe-worthy to those of us who are used to being a lower grade version of ourselves – especially if we are used to making plans and not following through with them.

Goal: *Make a list of the people in your life who are do-ers and achievers. The people you know will support you no matter what and hold you accountable for achieving your goals. If you haven't told them about your plans and goals yet, you should make it a priority to do so, and let them* *know that you would appreciate their support in this new and exciting venture in your life!*

Cheryl Lacey Donovan

NOTES

Love Yourself

The second is this: 'Love your neighbor as yourself.' There is no commandment greater than these." Mark 12:31

To love yourself means to wholly accept yourself just as you are. Loving yourself involves knowing that you deserve your own time, patience, effort, and even forgiveness.

When you love yourself, you take care of yourself emotionally, physically, mentally, and spiritually.

Each of these areas are interdependent so you'll find that you feel most loved when you attend to each of them with care.

Your Physical Self:

Your physical appearance and condition says a lot about how you feel about yourself.

What kind of effort do you put into taking care of your body each day? Are you up to date on all your yearly doctor's appointments. Do you take your medications regularly? If you answered no to any of these questions, then it's high time that you started being intentional about your physical well-being.

AUTHENTIC MOMENT:

Among other things I do make sure I see my doctors annually for any checkups that may be necessary. MY struggle is in exercising on the regular. However, I do manage to make sure I get in 10.000 steps and 30 minutes of physical activity a day. It has been said that 10,000 steps are equivalent to 5 miles a day.

I also try to cook health meals that include each of the food groups. Heavy on the veggies. On occasion we like to do a Daniel fast that generally lasts 21 days and helps to reboot the digestive system.

Here are some ways you can show self-love by tending to your physical body:

Take more time with your appearance. Most of us could easily spend a few additional minutes during our shower, shave, makeup application, or hair styling.

Ask yourself: do you notice the condition of your skin each day? Or do you spend your brief minutes in the mirror thinking unkind things about your body? Maybe you could use the time you spend in self-critique doing nice things for yourself instead: a touch more make-up or a bit closer shave can go a long way toward feeling good about yourself.

If you want to demonstrate to the world that you love yourself, spend more time on the physical you. Take pride in yourself and in your appearance. You'll be glad of your efforts and others will notice too.

Make a change. Occasionally, do something different with your appearance.

Shave off your mustache or beard and see how you look.

Get a haircut and style it into that sassy hairdo picture you saved.

Change the color of your hair.

Consider trying out a new style of clothing.

You can even change your eye makeup. YouTube has lots of video tutorials for different looks.

When you alter something about your appearance, you demonstrate you're worth the time and effort it takes to try something new. Plus, it's refreshing. Even if you decide not to stick with a new look, trying one out for a day or a week can bring new zest to your life.

Put energy into yourself. Knowing you're worthy of your own energy is an important aspect of loving yourself. When you direct your attention toward something that's just for you, even if only for ten minutes a day, the message you send to yourself is that you're worth it.

Having a partner and a family can be a huge drain on your energy in an average day. Conserving at least some of your energy for yourself shows you care about you as much as you do your family.

Notice your physical "positives." Take a good, honest look in the mirror. Instead of focusing on what you'd change, draw your attention to what you like. Maybe it's your handsome chiseled chin or how you smile with your eyes.

Acknowledge to yourself what you're proud of physically. Maybe you've got long legs or a strong core. Perhaps you like of the curve of your waist or your 6-pack abs.

Take plenty of time to do your physical inventory to find attributes to love about yourself. To feel even better, think about how you can enhance your best features. As you learn more about and augment your positive physical attributes, you'll discover self-acceptance, and be well on your way toward self-love.

Sleep more. Unless you're one of the lucky ones, you're most likely on the short end of getting enough sleep. Strive for seven to eight hours each night to show love to yourself.

Acknowledge that obtaining proper rest and sleep is on your priority list. And related to item #3, above, the more sleep you get the more energy you'll have. And that means more enthusiasm and love to give to your family and to yourself.

Brighten up. Wear a color you've never worn before. Something as simple as stepping up your wardrobe a bit indicates that you love yourself. Whether it's a blazer in that new dark teal shade or a print shirt that looks fresh, break into a new color scheme to show you're worth the effort to experiment with new ideas.

Ask yourself what your body requires. Perhaps for the first time in your life, seriously ask yourself what type of nourishment your body really needs. If you don't know, see a nutritionist. It's worth the cost of one or two office visits to find out what your body requires to be as healthy as possible.

If you already know what your physical self needs, apply your knowledge. Feed your body what it requires. Making your body a priority is a wonderful and important way to show love to yourself.

Consistently focus on your physical self. If your doctor approves, exercise in some form at least five days a week. Your body will feel better and better over time. Take some time to familiarize yourself with the flexibility of your limbs, the strength of your body's core, and the shape and efficiency of your muscles.

Strive to perform well physically in some specific way, whether it's doing calisthenics, yoga, weight-lifting, or jogging. Experiment with dance or try training for a triathlon. You'll be pleasantly surprised at the feelings of pride, confidence, and care you feel for yourself when you consistently focus on your physical body.

Acknowledge what your body does for you. One aspect of loving yourself is realizing everything your body allows you to do. Your mobility, your ability to use your hands to manipulate objects, and the energy that sustains you through a challenging day are all thanks to your body.

Your physical self holds up for you under plenty of pressure on any given day. Cultivate gratitude for how your body does pretty much everything you require. Love your body.

Show commitment to loving yourself. Through your behaviors every single day, be dedicated to fully accepting yourself. The level at which you ensure that you meet all of your physical requirements helps illustrate how you feel about yourself. Commit to your own self-care.

Tending to your body is one of the primary ways of showing how much you love yourself. Fortunately, there are plenty of ways to demonstrate that you love your body, and there's no need to do all of them in any given day, though you'll feel great if you do.

"We must be our own before we can be another's."
–Ralph Waldo Emerson

Your Intellectual Self:

Loving yourself also involves providing your brain with plenty of intellectual stimulation. Here are some effective ways to demonstrate self-love by giving your mind a workout.

Do something you've longed to do. Loved writing in high school? Always wanted to write a book? Now's the time to go for it. Exploring a new or long-loved subject might feel like a delicious indulgence. You deserve to feast your mind on subjects that are intellectually stimulating to you.

The internet offers an abundance of fascinating information. Dive into a search on a topic that arouses your interests.

Write down your life priorities. What's important to you? Next, jot down your life goals. What do you really seek to accomplish in life? Finally, take note of how you spend most of your time. Your three lists should all be similar or closely connected.

When you spend your time and thoughts on working toward your goals, your mind will be at its happiest and most fit. Plus, this sort of work shows that you care enough about yourself to have your priorities in good order.

Foster your passions and dreams. Ask yourself, "What do I care intensely about?" Then, delve into that subject. Learn everything you can about it. Practice it. Study it. Live it. If an idea, topic, or endeavor excites you, chase after it. The same goes for your dreams. Once you know what your hearts' desires are, do everything you can to achieve them.

Stay engaged with your life's passions and dreams. There's no better way to express self-love than to strive to give yourself what you truly want in life.

Ensure you've got a real life with real people. When you love yourself, you'll have close friends and family with whom you regularly spend time. Spend this time with your loved ones "in person" rather than with their Facebook pages.

Connecting with people in the physical world gives you many kinds of opportunities to keep your mind sharp. You'll engage in interesting discussions, be exposed to what's going on in the world, and have a forum to formulate and share your own opinions and intellectual ideas.

Avoid doing things just because "it's always been this way." Know and connect with your own consciousness. Perform behaviors deliberately and with great forethought. Living consciously shows that you use your mind to think through what you do because you care about what's going on in your life.

When you live intentionally, you intellectually consider the ramifications of the choices you make. You recognize how precious time is and judiciously spend the twenty-four hours you get in a day on what's most important to you. Now that's real self-love.

Take a personal inventory of your life. Make a list of your personal characteristics. Then take a piece of paper. Draw a line down the middle. On the left side, write down what's working. On the right side, write down what's not working. Then, make some decisions about the things you want to change. And then work on them.

This exercise will help you determine what your "thinking self" requires. Figuring out what you need to be intellectually challenged and move forward in life demonstrates that you're worth the time and effort to be happy.

Consider the bigger picture. As Mahatma Gandhi once said, "Be the change you want to see in the world." Use your mind to ponder how you want your life and the lives of others to be. Strive to behave the way that you hope others will behave. Consciously decide to make the changes that you hope other people will make. Set an excellent example to the world.

You may wonder how this can be considered self-love, since these actions may seem so intent on affecting other people. But how can you not feel good about yourself when you're focused on making the planet a better place?

Tell yourself you're worthy. Recognize that you deserve to be loved, not only by yourself, but by those around you. Mentally prepare yourself for the love you receive from others and yourself. Know that you're worth of all the love you give to yourself. With the proper mindset, your possibilities in life are limitless.

Working with your belief in yourself will help pave the way to more self-acceptance and self-love in other areas. You'll find loving yourself to be much easier when you're confident that you're worth the effort.

Find your power. When you see that you have control over your own mind, you'll be provided with opportunities to do as you wish with your life. In other words, you'll get to exercise the power you have in ways that enrich your existence.

Closely related to finding your power is infusing knowledge into your daily life. When you gain knowledge, you gain power. Accessing the power, you have in your mind means you'll experience self-confidence and feel love for yourself each day.

Loving yourself means you seek, find and experience all types of mental stimulation. You investigate topics of interest, maintain real friendships with real people, live consciously each day, consider the bigger picture, and find power within you.

Express your self-love by feeding your mind with intriguing thoughts, ideas and activities.

"At this very moment, you may be saying to yourself that you have any number of admirable qualities. You are a loyal friend, a caring person, someone who is smart, dependable, fun to be around. That's wonderful, and I'm happy for you, but let me ask you this: are you being any of those things to yourself?"

–Phillip C. McGraw, The Ultimate Weight Loss Solution: The 7 Keys to Weight Loss Freedom

Your Emotional Intelligence

Possibly the single most important facet of loving yourself is taking great care of your emotional self. What you believe to be true about yourself illustrates the degree to which you love and accept yourself.

Try these tips to love yourself more by taking care of your emotional being:

Accept yourself. Realize that you're as important, special and worthy as every other human being on earth. Connect deeply with this reality.

Use this as an affirmation: "I am important, special and worthy." Try saying the affirmation out loud. Repeat it. Write it down. Then, read it to yourself. Do this twice per day, once in the morning and once in the evening. Watch for subtle shifts in the way you view yourself.

Journal. Write in a journal about what you really like about yourself. (yes, the journal again)

Journaling helps you connect with your strengths. The time you spend writing down your thoughts is an opportunity to cultivate positivity about your best qualities. On an emotional level, you can most easily relate to positive feelings about yourself when you recognize your own strengths.

Claim responsibility for your own life. Often, we try to find external reasons for why something happened, such as, "Why does he keep hurting me?" or, "What makes her think I deserve this treatment?" Instead, take responsibility.

Ask yourself, "Since I'm responsible for myself, what do I need to do right now to remedy this situation for me?"

Once you claim responsibility for your own life, you'll fully consider the ramifications of your choices to stay in less than ideal situations. Over time, you'll begin to make decisions to disconnect from people, places and things that consistently harm you in some way.

Take the time to consider what's best for you in life. This is an enormous expression of the love you have for your own self.

Avoid negativity toward yourself. A person who loves herself avoids sending herself negative messages.

You can practice avoiding negativity and still acknowledge that no one is perfect. Being human doesn't mean that you deserve scorn, shame, or ridicule. Instead of beating yourself up emotionally, direct your energies toward turning any situation into something positive.

Forgive others. You'll feel less burdened by unwanted negative feelings when you cultivate forgiveness.

Of course, it's also okay to decide that even though you forgive someone, continuing to be involved with that person isn't healthy for you. When you forgive them first, however, you can move on without the extra emotional baggage of hurt and angry feelings.

Send out positive vibes to others. Show other people how loving, caring and kind you are. Often, we get immersed in our daily grind and don't notice all the opportunities we have to make someone's day. Showing positivity and kindness toward everyone can be intensely refreshing. When you do this, you make it obvious to others that you love yourself.

Say you're sorry if you are. Notice within yourself when you've made an error or had a misstep. Then, openly acknowledge it. This shows you're a genuine, caring human being.

You'll ultimately feel very good about apologizing when it's required. Saying you're sorry is a deeply satisfying experience that will help you to love and respect yourself even more.

Let go of any negative feelings you hold toward others. Cleansing yourself of as much negativity as possible sets you up for success in life. You feel better emotionally and physically, act more openly toward others, and demonstrate love to yourself. Lighten your emotional load by letting go of negativity.

Have self-respect. Refuse to allow anyone to emotionally harm you. Set guidelines within yourself about tolerating unsavory treatment from others. Having limits and boundaries is healthy and shows that you protect and respect yourself in all situations.

If you dislike the way someone treats you, leave their presence, if possible. Doing so will be the gateway toward re-claiming your self-respect and self-love.

Exit negative relationships, regardless of how scary that may feel. Ultimately, your love for yourself will be stronger than for someone who's less than positive toward you.

Understanding and acknowledging your own feelings validates your existence. By being honest with yourself about your feelings and acting in accordance with them, you honor and show love to yourself.

Your Spiritual Self: Caring for Your Soul

Filling your spirit with genuine joy is a must if you love yourself. Give yourself time to do only what you love to do. Try refreshing your living space even in small ways from time to time, disengaging from technology periodically, and doing other activities that bring adventure and joy into your life.

Check out these strategies and be inspired to think of still more ways to demonstrate how you care about yourself:

Make it a good morning. Take a little time in the morning to do something you really like to do. It might be 45 minutes of yoga to start your day off right. Maybe you'd like to read your favorite novel for 15 minutes before the kids get up. Or perhaps 10 minutes to practice meditation would give you the restful start you need to have a good day. Prayer is always a good choice.

Give yourself the gift of the first few minutes of each morning. Your whole day will be better, and your soul will thank you for that little bit of "me time" when you first arise.

Indulge. Do a little something special for yourself each day. You'll enjoy life more when you put in the effort to do just that one thing that makes your heart sing. Go ahead and do those activities you think are special, fun or self-indulgent.

You can afford 30 minutes to 1 hour every day just for yourself, can't you? Knowing you deserve it translates into loving yourself.

Change your personal space. Making small but meaningful changes in your home truly invigorates your soul. Nothing says "I love myself" like renewing your cherished space in your house.

Clean something deeply and well.

Throw some things away that weigh you down.

Rearrange the furniture in your living room. If you don't spend much time in your living room, try this in your favorite room, the one in which you hang out the most.

Paint. Write. Make music.

Turn on the tunes. Listen to your music each day for at least 15 minutes. Most phones today have MP3 players or iPods in them.

Turn off the gadgets. One day every other week, or even once a month, turn off your cell phone, television and computer. Disconnecting from your technology is a great way to re-connect with your soul.

Consider how you might spend a whole day away from all your gadgets. Will you take a walk, bake bread from scratch, or have a relaxing afternoon out in your yard? Maybe you'll spend the day with your father or your niece. Whatever you do with your unplugged time, you'll feel relaxed and rejuvenated.

Allow yourself to feel love from others. Experiencing the loving messages given to you by your family members and cherished friends is good for the soul. For example, when you go out to lunch with your sisters, savor their presence. Take in how they smile and make eye contact with you, or revel in that special silent communication you have.

Soak up the love that your cherished friends and family provide by staying emotionally in touch with their compliments or by their presence. Although we are often taught not to accept compliments or take them to heart, they're good for you, and are given with love. Accepting them is a way of loving yourself.

Worship. If you enjoy attending a church, temple, or other place of worship, doing so regularly is good for your soul. If you prefer to pray at home alone, that method of worship will also bring you soulful comfort and demonstrate self-love.

Perhaps you seek to discover the "right" place of worship for you. That's okay, too. Finding your spiritual "home" can be a great adventure in self-love.

People who want to worship and are successful in finding the place that fits for them re-fill their souls every time they attend the services or events that are meaningful to them.

If you have a religion or spirituality that's meaningful in your life, practice it. Many people report that worshipping simply makes them feel better.

If you don't have a spiritual "home," and feel like something's missing in your life, visit various kinds of churches to see if you can fill the void and discover what your soul seeks. Whether you go alone or with friends, you'll have fascinating experiences. And even if you don't find a place for you, you'll learn a lot about yourself.

Immerse yourself in nature. Make special efforts to experience the joys and beauties of nature. If you've ever walked through a pine tree forest, you know the awesome spiritual power inherent in the great outdoors.

Whether you put on your snowshoes and tromp off through piles of lovely white fluff or walk along a sandy beach somewhere collecting seashells, find a way to stay involved with nature.

Be adventurous. Find that part of you that seeks the unknown and strives for the yet-experienced adventure. Maybe you want to climb a mountain, run a sprint triathlon, or visit the pyramids in Egypt. Whatever your adventuresome spirit seeks, try to provide it in some way. You'll feel deeply alive and loved when you do.

Recognize that time is of the essence. Spend your hours and minutes in ways that demonstrate your self-love. Consider time as precious, golden moments meant to be spent doing the things you love and working toward your life's goals. Decide to love yourself every single minute of every single day by making each of those moments count.

Taking care of your spiritual self can be done by practicing one or many of the above strategies. Anything that brings joy to your soul ultimately demonstrates self-love.

"Your soul is all that you possess. Take it in hand and make something of it!"

–Martin H. Fischer

If you want to live a rich, full, authentic life, learn now to love yourself. Take care of all of your needs. When you love yourself, you're more likely to be loved by others and to be able to truly care for another person. Love yourself first and you'll experience the incredible joys that life can bring.

"It's important to talk about loving yourself and looking at your tragedies and the stuff that makes

Cheryl Lacey Donovan

you   grow."   –Anne   Heche

Visit http://www.cherylspeaks.org and click on our freebies page to take our self- care assessment test

In him we have obtained an inheritance, having been predestined according to the purpose of him who works all things according to the counsel of his will, Ephesians 1:11 ESV

Do you wake up each day dreading the idea of spending another day at work? You might even feel the need to be a part of something bigger and more meaningful. If you've failed to discover and build your life around your life purpose, you might feel dissatisfied with your life. Determining the purpose of your life can be a simple process.

It can take a bit of work to uncover the truth, but it's within you. It's waiting to be unearthed and utilized.

Living a life that's congruent with your purpose will allow you to start each day with a smile, hope, and a plan. It's a tool for connecting with something meaningful outside yourself. Everyone has a different "why". The trick is to determine the "why" that fits your values and talents.

If your life is in a rut, discovering your life purpose is the first step to a life filled with passion and contentment.

"The purpose of life is to live it, to taste experience to the utmost, to reach out eagerly and without fear for newer and richer experience."

- Eleanor Roosevelt

The Benefits of Discovering and Living Life on Purpose

Life purpose is that push that we need to make life more meaningful. Without purpose we aimlessly wader through life searching for meaning. Work is just work and there is no joy, no direction, and no destination.

The advantages of knowing your life purpose are far reaching:

1. You'll enjoy focus and clarity. Knowing your purpose helps you to hone in on those things that are most important to you. By doing so you can make better decisions about the people, places, and things you allow into your life.

2. It enhances your passion for life. Spending your day on the things that are most important to you will release your passion. You'll feel the enthusiasm you had as a child. With a compelling future and a high level of motivation, you become unstoppable. This is missing from a life without a clear purpose.

4. You become part of something bigger than yourself. You'll have sense of certainty that's both comforting and peaceful. It's a chance to make a big and meaningful contribution to the world.

Discovering the answer to the question, "What is the purpose of my life?" will change your life forever.

Now, let's see if we can explore purpose.

"The human race is a monotonous affair. Most people spend the greatest part of their time working in order to live, and what little freedom remains so fills them with fear, that they seek out any and every means to be rid of it."

- Johann Wolfgang von Goethe

Revealing Your Life Purpose

Self-reflection is one of the best ways to identify purpose, but you must ask the right questions. The responses to these questions will provide the answers you seek. However, it's imperative to listen to the answers because the responses you receive can be very subtle and quiet. Keep an open mind.

Be sure to record your answers!

Purpose questions:

1.   If you only had a year to live, how would you spend it?

2.   How do you want others to remember you? What would you like your obituary to say? How would you like your children, friends, and other family members to remember you?

3.   What did you love to do as a child that you no longer do? What have you given up over the years?

"Can I make enough money at this to have a decent lifestyle?"

4.   What type of discomfort can I handle? Everything is awful part of the time. Living your life's purpose will have its disadvantages. What can you handle?

5.   What topics and activities make you lose track of time? Have you ever gotten so involved with a conversation or an activity that you missed a meal or were amazed by how much time had passed?

6.   What do you dream about doing but are too afraid? Why haven't you taken the first step?

7.   How could you best serve the world? Of all the challenges that exist in the world, how could you best solve one of them?

Did you ask yourself every question? Did you record your answers?

How can you use these answers to enhance your life?

Introspection is a necessary part of finding your life purpose. Ask yourself the important questions and listen to the answers.

A small change can make a big difference. You are the only one who can make our world a better place to inhabit. So, don't be afraid to take a stand."

- Ankita Singhal

Writing for Purpose

Most of us don't enjoy writing. We'd much rather think things through, but writing can be a very powerful tool. In fact, it was one of the most cathartic things I ever did. There's just something about putting your thoughts and ideas on paper that can change your entire perspective. It provides clarity and focus. Pull out your journal and put pen to paper.

AUTHENTIC MOMENT: When I was led to write my first book it was simply to tell my story and perhaps help other women in the process of my transparency. I had no idea how cathartic it would be. It brought up so many feelings and emotions that I thought were long gone. I was able to deal with some fears, resentments, and disappointments in a way that was freeing and brought me peace. The bonus? I found my joy for writing again. That's right. Writing was one of the things I had given up (except for journaling) When I was younger I wrote poetry and short stories, but I gave that up to focus on a career in the medical field. My writing brought me full circle to my passion which is teaching and mentoring whether it's through my books, my speaking, or my media broadcasts, this is what I love to do. My passion.

Writing is a powerful tool that can permit a dialog with your subconscious:

1.   Use pen and paper or your computer to write down your thoughts. It doesn't need to make sense. Just write what comes to mind. You can write about your day. You can write about a situation. It doesn't matter. Write whatever comes to mind. You might think, "This is a dumb idea." That's fine. Write it down and avoid judging any of your thoughts. Just write.

2.   Empty your mind of your preconceived ideas. Part of the reason you've been unable to discover the purpose of your life is your flawed thinking. We limit

ourselves far too much. The answers often lie in places we never bother to look. Keep an open mind.

3. Expect that it will take 15 minutes to rid yourself of your mental clutter.

4. Stick with the process. At some point, you'll want to quit or do something else instead. There's no reason to be fearful of learning the truth. Fight through the discomfort.

5. Continue writing until you find it. How will you know? You'll know. You'll probably even cry. Just keep writing until you're certain you've found it.

› Go with the answer that provides the greatest emotional surge.

Before you start make sure you won't be interrupted. Most people that attempt this exercise will quit before reaching the end. Be one of the few that completes the process.

Thoughts about Meditation

Scripture tells us to meditate on the Word day and night. The secular world has begun to use medically and even in prisons but it's not a new concept.

I choose to meditate on scriptures that focus on who I am in Christ as well as those that pertain to a prayer or issues I may have at the time. For me the most important thing is to also wait for an answer. Often, Meditation is an acquired skill that requires time and effort to master. There's no better time to get started than today.

Use meditation to reveal your life purpose:

1. Sit comfortably in a quiet place free of distractions.

2.	Maintain a focus on your breath. Feel the air moving in your nose and out of your mouth. Continue doing this for at least 10 minutes.

›	Maintaining a focus on your breath is much more challenging than you think! Your mind will wander constantly. There's no cure other than practice.

3.	Ask yourself, "Why am I here? What is my purpose in life?" Then relax and listen to the answers in your Spirit.

4.	Repeat this process each day. It might take a few days to discover the answer. Meditate on a regular schedule and continue to ask yourself the appropriate questions. Continue the process until you receive an answer that makes intuitive sense to you. It will simply feel "right".

"The crowning fortune of a man is to be born to some pursuit which finds him employment and happiness, whether

it be to make baskets, or broadswords, or canals, or statues, or songs."

  - Ralph Waldo Emerson

Continuing the Quest for Purpose

Meditation and writing can be highly effective, but some of us have greater success with more conventional means.

Spend a few minutes on each question before moving on to the next:

1.   What are your greatest regrets? Which missed opportunities do you regret the most? Is there a skill you wish you had started learning years ago? What decisions would you change if given a second chance?

2.   Who inspires you the most? Think about the people that fill you with feelings of respect and admiration.

3. What are your natural talents? In what areas have you always excelled? Do you understand complex ideas? Is it your social skills? Are you musically talented? Are you compassionate and considerate?

4. What makes you feel good about yourself? If you could spend most of your time doing things that make you feel great, your life would be wonderful!

5. If you had to teach a subject, what would you choose? It's only enjoyable to teach subjects that you like. The subject you'd like to teach is a good candidate for your life purpose.

6. In what areas do people ask you for help?

7. Imagine you're 80-years old. What memories do you want to have? Imagine you're sitting on your front porch swing. What would you like to claim as your past? What type of relationships would you like

to have experienced? What do you want to have accomplished?

You now have a good idea of your life purpose. The next step is determining how to incorporate the knowledge into authentic living.

"As the struggle for survival has subsided, the question has emerged: survival for what? Ever more people have the means to live, but no meaning to live for."

- Viktor E. Frankl

Make Your Purpose a Part of Your Life

It's great that you've narrowed down your primary reason for living, but how can you use that knowledge? Knowledge is power but it's worthless if you're not applying it. Focus on making small changes that honor your purpose daily. Slow and steady wins the race when creating major change in your life.

1.   Look to the future. What does the end of your journey look like?

2.   What can you do today to get started? Starting is always the hardest part. What can you do today?

3.   Remind yourself of your purpose each day. Each morning and evening take a minute to remind yourself of your purpose. Look to the future and feel excited. This is especially important on those challenging days that inevitably happen from time to time.

4.   Track your progress. Keep a journal (I told you I liked to journal) and list your successes and failures. How can you experience more successes and prevent future failures? Appreciate how far you've come.

5. Spread the word. If you've found your purpose in life, it's your obligation to let the world know about it. How can you communicate the

importance of adult illiteracy to the world? You're not just a worker on this project. You're also a messenger.

Realize that making a big difference requires you to do the work. Avoid letting the magnitude of your dreams overwhelm you. A little work and attention each day will become cumulative. Your progress will shock you!

"It is not that we have so little time but that we lose so much. ... The life we receive is not short but we make it so; we are not ill provided but use what we have wastefully."

- Seneca

Finding your life purpose creates a course correction for your life. If you haven't taken the time to determine the purpose of your life, the quality of your experience on Earth has been limited.

Use every method at your disposal until you're satisfied with the answer you receive. I have written several affirmation/reflection workbooks that can help you with the process.

Today, more than ever, it's possible to make a living doing a wide variety of things. There is a way to make a living while being true to your life purpose.

Find your purpose and reclaim your life.

PUTTING IT ALL TOGETHER TO LIVE AN AUTHENTIC LIFE IN PURPOSE ON PURPOSE

Living authentically has never been so simple. Every chapter in this book has been written to outline something that you can use to develop your passions and become the best version of yourself possible.

You can bring the spark of your passion forward with every step you take forward in your day. Structure is the key to success, and if you can utilize it in your life, you will have no excuse not to live in authenticity.

The best way to begin is by examining what you want to accomplish and carving out the time to do so. What is your week going to look like? What about your month?

Making large end-goals to work toward can make it easier to break those goals into smaller pieces, ultimately providing yourself with a good framework with which to get things done.

But don't just write your goals down. Take actionable steps every day that will help you accomplish what you are trying to achieve.

It's important to understand that sometimes, life simply gets in the way of structures and plans, but that doesn't mean that you should give up on structure altogether. Instead of getting discouraged when you can't follow through on your goals for the day, maybe determine exactly what it was that caused the hold up and make a note of it so that you can do better next time. Simply reschedule the goal that you couldn't follow through, so you can get it done later. Never give up!

It is only when you stop trying that you lose your power. But with a resolve of steel and the structure to get you there, there will be no stopping you from living an authentic life!

Goal: *At the end of the month, sit down and envision where you want to be at the end of the month that is approaching. Write out daily, weekly, and monthly goals on a calendar that you will have regular access to. Do the same thing at the beginning of each week, especially if you are still trying to get in the habit of having a structured daily routine. Having a foundation to work from will make it that much easier for you to achieve your dreams and become the master of your destiny!*

Cheryl Lacey Donovan

NOTES

CONCLUSION

Every single one of us has a vision for our future No matter what that looks like, there are steps each of us can take to make our dreams of the future into something tangible.

We are all capable of taking the steps that we need to take to become the best versions of ourselves. Although it can be a challenge, there is nothing that a dedication to our own self-improvement can't solve. Every improvement, no matter how small, can help us to move mountains and achieve things we may never have believed possible before.

If you want to live in purpose on purpose, by following the advice in this book, you will find yourself well on the way to the authenticity you may have been too afraid to pursue before your awakening. It is more than just possible to live authentically; it is vital. We were each born with a special purpose, with talents and passions that were finely tuned to creating a better world. If we aren't doing everything in our power to see those passions translate into our reality, then the truth is that we are not only robbing ourselves, but we are robbing the rest of the world of the beauty that only we can bring into it.

Fortunately, if you have made it this far into the book, then you will know by now that you are more than capable of living an authentic life in purpose and on purpose. Like Nike says, "just do it!"

If you're looking for additional help and inspiration as you begin the process of authentic living, I would highly encourage you to check out my authentic living system at www.cherylspeaks.org/e320institute/can-i-be me .

Just so you know, the people that I enjoy working with are as follows:

- Purpose driven
- Like accountability
- Enjoy motivational reminders
- Don't quit
- Follow instruction
- Do the work

Getting in on this course will be one of the best investments you will ever make in yourself. My program will provide you with tangible takeaways, many of which could not be addressed in this book.

If living authentically is something you want to achieve, then we really should connect. If you want to learn to be yourself around others, to live your life according to what's important to you, to crate and authentic ministry or business, to live and speak your truth, to identify your purpose, or to lead with authenticity, enrolling in one of the Can I Be Me Programs can help.

I've created a free 4 video training session for those who are committed to living authentically in purpose and on purpose. You can access the free training at http://www.cherylspeaks.org/can-i-be-me/free-training. You will also find additional information about the authentic living program there.

Regardless of whether you enroll in the program, I would be grateful if you would share your progress with me.

Let me know what you're doing on the journey to authenticity and how it has transformed your life. Reach out to me at cheryl@cherylspeaks.org

Thank you for reading my book. I appreciate your feedback and would love to hear what you have to

Can I Be Me?

say. Please leave me a review on Amazon. Always grateful!

Limited Special Offer:

Can I Be Me? Course

This course can be done as a self-paced home study course, an online course, or a group coaching course

For More Information Visit

http://www.cherylspeaks.org/E320institute/can-i-be-me

Made in the USA
Lexington, KY
06 June 2018